An Animals' Charter

An Animals' Charter

Noël Sweeney

This edition was first published in Great Britain in 2020
by Alibi an imprint of Veritas Chambers
Unit 4 + 1 BP Bristol

A catalogue record for this book is available from the British Library.

ISBN 978-1-872724-12-6

Printed in Great Britain by
CPI Group (UK) Ltd, Croydon CRO 4YY

Dedication

To Wendy and Maureen and Polly all of whom were there at the start and stayed right until the end. They showed that buttered parsnips are no substitute for deeds.

Acknowledgements

For the mighty guidance provided by the pure vision of Lewis Gompertz and Henry Salt who opened my eyes to what matters in the world. Together they provided a map and the sign and the moral compass to find the roots of the route.

In remembrance of Helen Jones and Tom Regan who realised that when it comes to speaking for those who rely on you to be their voice that whatever the question it is never answered by a false compromise.

May I add a one hand clap for Henry Holzer whose fiery fist held a torch that lit the darkness of animals' lives.

Contents

1

Thinking about Things

God is so wise that when she created birds she gave them complete freedom from the chains of the sky. We are so wise that we prove our love of birds by confining them in cramped cages.

Bo Diddley sang with his mesmeric rasping blues plea for understanding by his lover claiming, 'You can't judge a book by the Cover'. While no one would wish to doubt the evergreen Diddley, that is untrue here as species of the grebe portrayed were hunted to death by vainglorious women seeking fine feathers for their snook-cocked hats.

Cages and covers have a connection when you consider how we condemn other species for no other reason than that is what they are by birth. Human rights are beyond price because without them people cannot live and die freely with dignity. Equally without them people are fettered by the chains of law and subjugation. Animal rights are the same for the same reason.

Racism is evil because it devalues and prejudges people without a valid cause. Sexism is base as it discriminates against humans purely as a matter of biology. Speciesism originates from a similar source as racism and sexism. Yet it is worse as a form of prejudice because animals need us to resist our prejudice. Animals are denied legal rights because they are hamstrung by being denied a human tongue.

The connection between racism and sexism and speciesism is they are bound together by our bond of bias. The arguments we base on race and sex, including biological differences and inferiority and intelligence, are equally applicable to animals. Why then do most human victims of personal prejudice fail to identify with their animal counterparts? You may well ask why self-proclaimed feminists feel it is fine to shaft animals by eating and wearing them? Is that the spirit of Wollstonecraft? You might ask why religious zealots practise their sacred beliefs by sacrificing animals? Is it simply that we can use and abuse those unable to climb the first rung of our legal ladder?

Animals are our victims before birth and only cease being so after their death. For our actions against animals are prejudicially sutured within the sinews of our society. Law as the only social instrument that could and should protect their rights deny them a role and status. Instead we vicariously dilute their position and limit their power by claiming to promote their welfare. We prefer 'welfare' to granting animals 'rights' as it allows us to continue to take advantage of our strength relative to their vulnerability and weakness.

Over two hundred years ago the poet Soame Jenyns identified the butcher as a reflection of his work and our lack of feeling: 'The butcher knocks down the stately ox with no more compassion than the blacksmith hammers a horse-shoe, and plunges his knife into the throat of an innocent lamb with as little reluctance as the tailor sticks his needle into the collar of a coat.' Then as now legally the horse is no different than the steel shoe that shod her feet or indeed the knife that took her life.

That is why in 2020 we still legally classify an animal in the time-immemorial phrase as a *'thing'*. That they bleed and breathe is conveniently forgotten if that fact clashes with our preternatural greed and need for profit. We ignore the fact they have a heartbeat and a pulse for the same reason. Our view is shaped and shared by a natural conspiracy where all humans take advantage of all animals for no other reason than just because we can.

That focus is sharpened when you consider 'Castaway', a television programme for general consumption, where the contestants had to breed and kill their own animals. Why? There is no reason except that it appeals to the viewer plus who among the victims can object to their fate? Given that that was 20 years ago, nothing has changed as now these crass 'reality' shows use the colloquial 'creepy crawlies' to scare contestants and amuse easily-pleased voyeuristic viewers. It is a small step away from the black and white minstrel shows and wife-selling auctions. Taking advantage of those creatures that are within our control is always a form of bullying. Similarly in 2020 we have 'Meat the Family' which is the same concept with the same format for the same reason. It would be unacceptable if it was now practised on a non-consenting human. No objection could be made by any of the actual victims as by then the animals were just more statistics of misery as the main meal.

As it involves the 'family' rather than an anonymous animal abuser, the viewer has the advantage of seeing their collective palate as the yardstick by which they jointly decide to kill and eat their 'pet'. The lesson that animals have no value beyond being human food is underlined by the mother preparing and sharing the bodies of those pets. The echoing laughter around the table verifies the value of the social occasion. Children as viewers and better still as part of the family, immediately learn the life lesson that animals have no value as living creatures.

Then in 2020 a Chinese entertainment company threw a pig to the ground in a bungee jump. The Chinese crowd 'laughed and jeered' while the falling pig was 'squealing in terror'. The company claimed it was 'just fun, entertainment'. If it is such 'fun' why are their employees not trussed up with their feet bound and then forced off exactly as the victim pig was by them? The 'fun' was finished when the tortured pig was duly slaughtered. That start and end did not seem such fun as to touch the humans' funny bone making them wish to share in it.

Similarly in 2020 a chef, Niklas Ekstedt, extolled the virtues of eating live creatures: 'It freaks out my British friends when we toast bread over a flame, slather it in honey and then lay it on an ants nest. You wait for the ants to crawl over the toasts stick – especially the acidic fat red ones – and then eat them while they are writhing and wriggling! Delicious!'

No doubt a hedgehog between two hunks of Hovis or a slice of snake in a sourdough sandwich would be equally delicious to taste by people whose taste proves a lack of it. Perhaps even Ekstedt roasted and toasted over a barbecue cauldron would have a certain appeal for a discerning cannibal. Similarly Hirst placed a formaldehyde animal in a tank and live butterflies in a locked room with no means of escape to prove his natural artistry. The title of his Exhibition, 'In and Out of Love', shows that he fails to understand language too. During one of his experiments Hirst sacrificed 900 butterflies. All of it proves, as in so many aspects of our dealings with animals, it is problematic to distinguish a gifted latter-day Rembrandt from a practitioner of art with a capital 'F'.

The difference between us and animals to experience pain and pleasure is indivisible. Why then do we treat them with multiple-contempt on every moral and legal level? The answer is no less than our power over the powerless. Animals are our paupers at a rich man's table. All humans, however poor, are rich in comparison as animals are our paupers from birth onwards.

Legally the animals' lives and future count for nothing. They are not even social pawns in a political game. Animals are less than pawns because they are not part of our plan which is comprised of rules made by and for us. We decide who can share the benefit and who will bear the burden. We dictate the state of society's game plan so animals are bound by our ball and their chain.

Animals have no status in our society because we deny them what we possess: a legal 'personality'. As a result they are our subjects and subject to our rules. English law does not recognise animals worthy of possessing an 'artificial personality' which is how we classify commodities such as icons and heritage items. Lacking even that artificial personality renders an animal's voice as valueless as a dead ventriloquist's dummy. Animals always were and still are our artefacts.

The first major animal welfare legislation in the world was introduced in England in 1822 by an Irish barrister, Richard '*Humanity Dick*' Martin. The statute, known colloquially as 'Martin's Act', was the benchmark the SPCA used when it was formed in 1824. In 1840 it was granted Royal patronage and became the RSPCA. As a group and social movement they knew that as fine words butter no parsnips, the law is the only way to protect animals from their suffering at human hands.

Martin explained the aim of that change was that, 'If legislation to protect animals is to be effective, it must be adequately enforced.'

Around that time Darwin opined that humans are only 'strategic monkeys.' He was wrong. Monkeys are entities of their own. They do not have to be compared to humans in order to gain an identity. They exist as entities because they exist. That is the way we weigh the relative role of humans. An identity is not better or worse by being compared to another living being. It is a valueless distraction to rely on a comparison however altruistic may be the motive. Darwin was well-intentioned, but misguided.

Animals are deemed to be different than us and inferior to us and liable to be abused by us because we have a choice and they have no voice. Unlike us, we presume that they do not have a soul. Although we cannot prove possession of a supposed soul is either absent or present for them or us, it does not matter in relation to our assessment of animals. For only by assuming that falsehood to be true, can we continue to abuse animals in society and at will and by law.

A dung beetle is as important and unimportant to the planet as a human. When the last human is dead the fimetic world will still exist. When the last dung beetle is dead, will the world disappear? We figure we are at the top of nature's ladder, when we are just part of the universe with most species being more vital to the continuation of the world than us. Thors Hanson went travelling with his son, Noah, on a journey to discover bees and ecology. Noah made an observation that so struck Hanson he had nothing to add. He made it the last sentence of his book, *The Buzz* [2018]: 'The world can live without us, but we can't live without bees.'

Although fox-hunting is now illegal in England, though still practised by some miscreants, the point made by Henry Salt is one we must grabble for the nettle of our inherent inhumanity and not be afraid to feel the sting of his sense: 'We have to decide, not whether the practice of fox-hunting, for example is more, or less, cruel than vivisection, but whether *all* practices which inflict unnecessary pain on sentient beings are not incompatible with the higher instincts of humanity.'

By comparison, in the *Hull Prison Riot Case* [1979] counsel for the defendant submitted that society was to be judged by how it treated its lowest members. The Court of Appeal agreed. Lord Justice Shaw said that although they were prisoners they still had rights as 'The courts are in general the ultimate custodians for the rights and liberties of the subject whatever his status and however attenuated those rights and liberties may be as a result of some punitive or other process.'

The principle is right. However, the unanimous judgment is wrong. Animals, not prisoners, are the lowest members of our society. How a society treats its weakest members reflects and determines its strength.

Are the weak to perish or be protected by the strong? It is a question to be resolved by compassion and compromise and conscience.

Why do we keep concentrating on animal 'welfare' when it has no lasting value to animals? Why do we adopt that approach when all our existing and proposed laws advance welfare rather than rights? Why do we use the term 'animal rights' as a pejorative one when applied to activists? Why is any struggle for human rights always applauded as a valid cause?

The reason is somewhat straightforward in that we rely on and introduce legislation to protect people under the guise of protecting the welfare of animals. Is our law biased against animals because it is biased in favour of us? That question is the reason for and theme of this book. All living beings that are human have an unassailable desire to be free. People whose liberty is restrained or denied have fought for their rights, sometimes fighting unto death for their right to live. That is because we place such value upon it in relation to others as well as ourselves. Why then should we not have the same feeling and wish to fight for the rights of others that share our planet? Why do we want to use and abuse animals for no other reason than purely because we can? Why should we wish to do so?

Given we use law to care for those who are disabled and different in some way to lessen their burden of discrimination, why do we willingly take advantage of animals? Why do we draft laws that advance injustice against those under our yoke when that is contrary to its moral purpose?

Law is our leveller that promotes the pursuit of justice. The worst crime a human being can commit against another human being is murder as it deprives the victim of the right to live. In the 16th century Leonardo said, 'I have from an early age abjured the use of meat, and the time will come when men such as I will look upon the murder of animals as they now look upon the murder of men.'

It is true that many of the points within the Animals' Charter are radical and revolutionary and indeed utopian. That does not mean that they are wrong. After all precisely the same arguments used against granting animals legal rights were used against the abolition of slavery by the slave traders. Who would now argue for slavery? For if you would then you equally have to be prepared for someone else to believe it would be a good idea to make you a slave. That is why human rights and animal rights are closely linked in being two sides of the same coin of compassion.

Any question we ask and answer we give about animals within our society and our abuse of them has to be predicated on the basis of Darwin's classic statement in the *Descent of Man*: 'There is no fundamental difference between man and the higher mammals in their mental faculties...The lower animals, like man, manifestly feel pleasure and pain, happiness and misery... Nevertheless, the difference in mind between man and the higher animals, great as it is, certainly is one of degree and not kind.'

Conversely we kill millions of animals in the most atrocious manner in our abattoirs everyday merely because the victims do not possess a vicarious Animals' Charter.

In *Swan* Mary Oliver asks the body-blow clincher question we must all ask ourselves: 'And have you too finally figured out what beauty is for? And have you changed your life?'

Yet where animals are concerned we have still not learned that in the seeds of their destruction we sow our own. It is further proof that they and we need An Animals' Charter.

Where animals are concerned China is one of the, if not *the*, cruellest country in the world. They have no respect for human rights, let alone animal rights. The pig dragged to the top of the tower and thrown off in a bungee jump was after all a Chinese Festival and merely part of their culture. So it is now profitable for our culture and indeed shareholders that China is one of our major trading partners in the world. As China eats any animal alive that can move towards death at their hands in their public markets, many experts consider the trade in wild animals is the main cause of transmitting the coronavirus in 2020. The Sars virus began in China 15 years ago for the same reason. The trade in wild animals, domestic and exotic, include badgers and bats and cats and dogs and hedgehogs and rats and snakes. Professor Diana Bell stated in 2020, 'The warnings were not heeded so here we are again. Now it's time for collective action to stop the illegal trade in wild animals, their continuing sale in markets across the region which mix a vast array of species and of course the pathogens they carry.'

Meanwhile thousands of people have died and many people have been infected on a universal level. The National People's Congress of China responded by placing an immediate ban on 'the consumption and trade of wild animals, in a fast-track decision designed to help stop the spread of coronavirus.' They followed it by announcing that 'Eating cats and dogs is to be outlawed in the southern China technology hub of Shenzhen as the country clamps down on the wildlife trade that scientists suspect led to the coronavirus outbreak.' On reflection they added that, 'Banning consumption of wild animals is a common practice in developed countries.' China did not identify the developed countries or specify how if at all it was one of them or they could ever be in that category.

The same day in February 2020 that that ban was announced, an octogenarian pensioner was sentenced to a suspended sentence of imprisonment for, following a long dispute, training her parrot to emit a screeching squawking sound to 'torment her neighbours'. The neighbours were forced to take action as the loud repeated operatic sound was 'akin to Chinese torture.' Perhaps it is just as well that it happened in Kent for if it was China the parrot's fate would have probably been to be a politician's breakfast.

All in all the only way to make progress with treating animals as living creatures is a defined change in the law. We showed the world the way in 1822 by introducing the first major legislation to 'protect' animals in relation to their 'welfare'. Meanwhile we have lagged behind other countries in respect of properly protecting animals. The way forward is by acknowledging and adopting the sound view of Salt in *Cruelties of Civilization* [1895]:

'It is only by the spread of the same democratic spirit that animals can enjoy the "rights" for which even men have for so long struggled in vain. The emancipation of men from cruelty and injustice will bring with it in due course the emancipation of animals also. The two reforms are inseparably connected and neither can be fully realised alone.'

Welfare as a concept is of little value to animals. Welfare might allow them to have a bigger cage or more links in a chain, but they are still subject to our terms during their lives. Rights are the only answer for all animals. Human rights guarantee people can live and die with dignity. Animal rights are denied by us though they are essential for the same reason. While there will have to be wide-ranging changes in favour of animals to incorporate those ideas and ideals in law, the major change that is initially essential is the appointment of An Animals' Advocate. That Advocate would have a duty and responsibility to introduce an Animal Rights Act and a legal personality for them. Those factors would recognise their sentience and that they are entities in their own right. Together these changes and more would guarantee the quintessence of natural justice that rights run with life itself. An Animals' Charter would reflect and respect that self-evident truth. The time for us to face our prejudice and change so we cannot meander is the challenge of our law making it suit both goose and gander. Given our present position the time for their future stance is long since past.

2

Power on Power

The Founding Fathers of America declared that 'all men are created equal' while excluding black people and every non-American not in their self-image. To them it was as natural as a master of slaves trading them as a sub-human species. Many signatories of the Declaration of Independence owned slaves. Those signatories saw slaves as 'property', just as we see animals and just like them without any legal rights. Of course it excluded all women too, white or otherwise. Their problem springs from the fact they based their ideas and ideals on English Law but conveniently ignored the crucial analysis of slavery within the principles of the common law.

We have forged a relationship with animals much as we have done with slaves. Given the choice we have chosen and continue to be parasitic rather than symbiotic. One moment we are willing to vivify them, next moment we are willing to kill them. We are content to ignore the impure truth that one woman's meat is another animal's death.

The principle we prefer not to dwell upon is that many members of our society are vulnerable because we deem them to be inferior. Our law then allows us to assume superiority over those in our clutches as by our conspiracy we gain control without any loss. When might is right we have the legal and moral benefit that the victim cannot resist our strength. We can use them in commerce, religion, science, sport and war. Then whoever they are, the last act our animal victims will do when completing their duty to us is to die on our terms.

Animals are alone within our society as being the only beings legally classified as things. Given their respective vulnerability it is no surprise that research in 2018 by the Massachusetts Institute of Technology involving over 2,000,000 people in over 200 countries on the 'moral decisions that driverless cars might have to resort to', there was 'emphatic global preferences' for 'sparing the lives of humans over the lives of other animals...preserving the lives of the young, rather than older people'. Evidence of a 'Link' between animal and elder abuse is related and well-established: each one becomes a victim because of their innate vulnerability. The four elements of that Link are animal abuse, child maltreatment, domestic violence and elder abuse.

Animals are a natural part of the fabric of our society. Whether they are a Great Dane or an Irish wolfhound, be they domestic or wild, on a farm or on a plate, in a laboratory or in us, animals touch our daily lives in every sense. As that includes the economic and political and social sense, it is bound to be reflected in the legal one too. Animals are inextricably connected with us, so naturally we use our power to control them by law.

3

Blinded by the Law

Indeed, rather than the reverse, animals are classified as our '*property*' so they can and do become victims within our legal system. Much as a shuttlecock child who can be moved from parent to parent and care home to foster home within our system, so can animals be subject to rules designed by us to take advantage of their lack of legal status.

Law is more important in relation to animals than it might at first glance appear to be. Ultimately law is a social tool that can be used on their behalf to rescue a 'rescued' dog who is wrongly sentenced to death or an abandoned horse starving in a mud-ridden field when the departing caravans leave the village green. The law can reach the dark recesses of an abattoir when 'whistle-blowers' reveal animal abuse which is concealed as there are no cameras there.

Animals have a certain undeniable claim within society to be treated as sentient living creatures deserving of being protected by law. That is not a grudging concession granted by some self-ordained superior being, but the recognition that law is the universal language that speaks for the vulnerable and the weak.

Isonomy guarantees the principle of equality within law that cannot be fudged or judged to exclude some people. There is a reason to believe that treating other beings as subject to the same noble ideals we seek enhances humanity and society. By lessening their suffering we can promote equality and pursue our ideal of justice. Whether the ideas and ideals have been achieved in practice depends upon how we have interpreted and used the law. This analysis will show to the reader if we have failed or succeeded in that search for justice. Even if justice is blind, we cannot conceal the truth.

4

Poetry of Legal Slavery

The reason for a lot if not most of the abuse we cause animals to suffer stems directly and indirectly from the belief that we have a soul. That belief separates us from them. Such a fact distinguishes humans from animals.

There is a slight problem with that self-perpetuating belief in the respect that it is based on a falsehood. Far from being a fact, that 'belief' leads us to claim to be superior to animals. Consequently we can then act accordingly in exercising our assumption. We use a false logic in all of our treatment of animals. Hence we defend the indefensible and justify the unjustifiable by a conspiracy that all humans share to a greater or lesser degree. We openly take advantage of two related limbs namely animals are vulnerable because they have no legal voice and we deprive them of having a legal voice.

We aim to continue to conspire against animals possessing a legal voice by our own silence. Our conspiracy of silence arises from the simple position that we all gain from the result. Our ability to take advantage of animals allows us to practise abuse as our legal *mores*.

The position of animals supposed lack of soul is examined in more detail and depth in Chapter 5. As that moral issue is the root of our legal problem, it relates to all aspects of how we abuse animals. Here these poems and songs analyse their position within our society highlighting the unequal balance between our greed and their need.

The unequal balance starts and ends with law. That is why English colonials figured it was morally acceptable in 1619 to 'buy' 20 Angolans who had been kidnapped by the Portuguese. The enslaved Africans that were bought in the British colony of Virginia on 20 August marked the start of slavery in the New World that lasted for 250 years – or more accurately, for 400 years. Our ancestors acted in that manner for these related reasons: they saw the black slaves as a trading commodity no different than animals; they could get away with it because the black slaves had no legal voice; the conspiracy of the traders usurped any compassion for the human cargo.

Animals in America were out in the cold and so beyond the consideration of the colonials. For that same climate of a lack of compassion for other creatures infiltrated the minds of the English throughout other colonies and continents and indeed the world. Animals were and are just our playthings, to be used and abused at will. Our mind-set is more than a habit. It is no less than an addiction. Animal abuse is ingrained in our daily living as natural as breathing.

Even those who oppose animal abuse and would never condone cruelty to them in any form would in the next breath reach for a hamburger or parade in a mink coat stolen from the first owner while she was still wearing it on her body. While we acknowledge some unpalatable aspects of animal abuse as undesirable, we still refrain from granting animals legal rights and a legal representative to protect their interests and ultimately their lives.

Research in 2019 has confirmed the connection between humans and animals such that the latter are or at least potentially 'our ancestors'. That research shows the connection between apes and chimpanzees and orang-utans and us. The scientific significance of that premise and conclusion is how it reflects on the Darwinian theory of evolution. On one level it affects our existing knowledge. Nevertheless it is vital that we concentrate on what matters regarding the legal role and status of animals. For on a salutary level whether orang-utans are the 'ancestors' of humans does not matter at all. Animals exist for their own interests and their own reasons. They are entities that live and die whether they ever have any contact with humans. We should reflect upon and respect that simple position as we wish to be valued in our own right. The only way that they are not victimized is by being the subjects of and subject to an Animals' Charter. A Charter prevents them being an object of our prejudice and promotes their presence as beings worthy of respect. A Charter prevents animals being our literal and legal scapegoats as it allows the protection afforded by a new label of law which confirms they are creatures entitled to dignity.

Animals do not depend on us to exist. Animals should not depend upon us to survive except within the honesty of the law. Animals have their own reasons and seasons outside of ours. Might is never right when it is used purely to deny another body the legal right to live.

All those factors and features play out in these shadow sketched epitaphs. They are meant to be spoken and sung so that finally you may be the animals' voice. That is the sound of harmony and justice and truth.

Rape of the Wild

It's a beautiful day
Let's go out and kill something

Hey children come and gather round
Lust is the lesson you will learn
From a whisper to a roar hear the sound
Of the season for killing and the reason our fire burns

Hey children come closer this time
Let the race towards his fate start
A thrill's a thrill and he's well past his prime
So soon you will see the scared stag's still-warm still-beating heart

There's a blood-red sky kissed by a passing cloud
Blood on the lips of the circus crowds
Blood on the teeth of the unleashed hounds
Blood in the bubble that traps his voice
Blood on the blade that destroys his choice
Blood on his forehead is the child's prize
Blood on our hands when the bullet flies
Matches the bloody fear-filled light from the hart's dying eyes

Hey children this is your moment
The price of life is a cheap death
Let this day stay and silently ferment
Within you so you will live your lust through the
beast's last breath

It's a beautiful day
Let's go out and kill truth

Here Comes L124

Here Comes L124
With our claw of the law
Hammering on your door
Nail all your lies to the court floor
We've got eyes on the prize and a mojo on the rise
Here Comes L124

No one's above the Law
And no one is below
Regardless of their fault or flaw
Law shields the lowest of the low
Each one counts an equal amount
No one's measured as minimal
Whether you're a king or a common criminal
Unless you happen to be born an animal

No one's above the Law
When we balance the scales
It's always an even see-saw
Justice succeeds when all else fails
Each one counts an equal amount
No one's seen as subliminal
Whether innocent or guilt-ridden criminal
Unless you happen to be born an animal

No one's above the Law
Regardless of their claim or fame
Whether you're a prince or cat's-paw
Justice treats everyone the same
Each one counts an equal amount
No one's weighed or made marginal
If you're a first timer or seasoned criminal
Unless you happen to be born an animal

All are equal in law's sequel
Our moral code is seminal
The only sin worse than being a criminal
Is the birthmark curse of being an animal

Here Comes L124
With our claw of the law
Hammering on your door
Nail all your lies to the court floor
We've got eyes on the prize and a mojo on the rise
Here Comes L124

My Forever Friend

Though you're gone from me never to return
The ashes of my heart burns and burns
Something you said with a look is the best lesson I
   learned
We have no time to lose or lie
In living and loving before we die

It's hard to know some things are meant to be
It was me for you and you for me
So I'm still mesmerised by your gypsy mystery
Though you tried so hard to explain
We two will never pass this way again
When the road was rough
When the times were tough
When I never had enough
You were everything and more to me
Sanctuary
Since your demise there's no time for dry eyes
How it was and is and always will be just you for me
Sanctuary
Only one had the skeleton key to reach the riff of my
   raff
You with your untamed beauty and wild country cat
   laugh

To hide a while behind the sad sweet smile
Knowing sadness is always in style
You unlocked the secret of every unsung song
Holding each moment way too long
For now alone together we belong
Sanctuary
We stood face to face to meet our last task
Sanctuary
There was no reason for any mask
Sanctuary
You were there at the start I was there at the end
My lodestar guide at every wend
My North Star and forever friend
Farewell my faithful feline friend
Last goodbyes under Somerset skies

A Prickly Thorn in the Hotel:

When Keith's wife died he ran the little B & B on his own in Cornwall. He was quietly proud of it as after service in the Marines he was keen to give his valued customers an excellent service.

He was a little angry when he visited my Chambers.

Old Keith asked me how he should draft a letter because he was really browned off with some posh jumped-up merchants and Bullingdon Boy-type bullies who irritated him to the core when they visited his Hotel in a leafy region of Falmouth for some Rag stunt or on a Stag weekend.

He showed me a letter from one such creep who asked Keith if it was 'O.K. if I bring the old mutt, Spike, along too as all the boys like a bit of fun with him. Though I know some down market hotels like yours don't like mutts?'

Keith was very upset and said he would 'give them a piece of my mind.' After a while I managed to calm him down and persuaded him to allow me to write it for him.

The letter from Keith said:

Dear Sir,

By all means bring Spike to us. We will be pleased to see him. We have a high regard for all dogs in this Hotel. Indeed I have never been woken in the middle of the night by a drunken dog that has lost his key and was intent on fighting the Head Chef or one who has puked up all over the new lounge carpet. We have never had any dog steal our towels or go to sleep with a cigarette dangling from their frothy lips so we were forced to call the Fire Brigade where they almost set the place on fire. May I add that I have never had a dog that cheated me when it came to paying for his board or tried to rape the chambermaid or insult the very even-tempered and personable owner.

So please send Spike to us and we will give him a moist bone and a very warm welcome.

Yours insincerely,

N. Sweeney

PS. If Spike will vouch for your conduct then you can come too.

Strike Some Sparks

Rubin Stacy sways in the breeze
Sheriff's men stare at his knees
Sheriff's men kick up the leaves
Rednecks loiter under the trees
Then they pulled the loose noose tight
His eyes popped and filled with fright
Rubin Stacy swings in the breeze
Stray dog suspended at his knees
Truth is always forged under fire
A mask won't change the face of a liar
Stacy and the stray couldn't win
Rubin was pinched and lynched for his ebony skin

Don't call me at all
I don't buy your lies
Save your second-hand stories
And don't try to philosophize
Just heed my need
A message that's short and stark
Only call me when you're going to
Raise some sparks for the ghost of Rosa Parks

Maya Angelou learned as a child
The smile of the paedophile
Was a leer meant to beguile
And break a mind free and fragile
Filling her with promised fear

Forced her voice to disappear
No less than a sin and a crime
Maya was betrayed for all time
Just a girl and her dog on the street
She heard the stalker's pounding feet
She heard the caged canary sing
Maya was broken without a prayer or a wing

Don't call me at all
I don't buy your lies
Save your second-hand stories
And don't try to philosophize
Don't call at all
Until your bite matches your bark
Only call me when you're going to
Raise some sparks for the soul of Rosa Parks

George was grabbed by stone cold Chauvin
A pack with a biased plan
Handcuffed George under their van
Bad blood while his race almost ran
George winced with each wave of pain
Chauvin burst his windpipe vein
George choked and cried 'please, I can't breathe'
Chauvin's death knell knee wove the wreathe
From 1619 'til its High Noon
America burns its biased moon
George Floyd was destroyed by the pack
Sentenced to death for the crime of being born black

Please don't shame my name
I'm deaf to your lies
I can't use your false excuse
And don't try to philosophize
Burn bright and right
A torch of truth our trademark
Only call me when you're going to
Raise some sparks for the heart of Rosa Parks

Let's poison all the honey bees
Think of the profit we'll seize
Keep spraying that pesticide
Let's destroy all the countryside
In the end it won't matter
Let the fat cats get fatter
Don't avoid ritual slaughter
Or avoid the polluted water
So let's all live high on the hogs
With 'no blacks, no Irish, no dogs'
Who cares and who counts the cost
8 million horses lost in our World War Holocaust?

A truth that don't offend
Is not one to defend
So just leave me alone
Let me pick another bone
Don't call at all
Unless you're ready to save the shark
Then call me when you're going to
Strike some sparks for the spirit of Rosa Parks

Strike some sparks for the ghost of Rosa Parks
Strike some sparks for the soul of Rosa Parks
Strike some sparks for the heart of Rosa Parks
Strike some sparks for the spirit of Rosa Parks

Liberation Drummer's Blues

Another cat another dog
Another horse another frog
Another hedgehog pinned to the table
A tiger paces his prison cage
The lion roars with a circus rage
Defeats all the dreams of the childhood fable

The current makes the stray bitch yelp
But she has no friend and no help
She's seen as a clockwork robot machine
Strap the macaque on the steel bench
He's a living tool, a monkey-wrench
Hands steeped in morphine we'll never scrub clean

The butcher's cleaver blow-by-blow
Echoes the sexy chef's screen show
When the butcher becomes a housewife
So she can cut her cute conscience
To forget their sense and sentience
She can see the chicken as just a stuffed Steiff

The truth so blunt it twists and turns
As sharp as the housewife's knife
Though she knows in her soul
That one man's meat is another animal's life

We want a taster for the King
For the comfort their death will bring
Let's splice the dice so we'll kill all the mice
We'll still end up winning the game
Without a sense of guilt or shame
Seeking a scapegoat as one more sacrifice

Circle of death in Parliament Square

London Town on a sunny day
Maggie Smith's eyes are filled with rain
London Town on a rainy day
Maggie Smith's eyes are filled with pain

London Town on a sunny day
Dave Jones' eyes are filled with rain
London Town on a rainy day
Dave Jones' eyes are filled with pain

Daisy was starving and stranded
A pregnant stray without a home
Another mother abandoned
Until Maggie threw her a bone

Then they shared their luck and their life
Together through the windswept rain
Sharing their food while dodging strife
Sharing love and each other's pain

Then bitter snow shards bit and burned
Through her fur and their flimsy clothes
The temperature fell and turned
Bones to ice so they dozed and froze

Three bodies in Parliament Square
Three bodies without a heartbeat
Three bodies there yet no one cared
Three more statistics on the street

Politicians stepped by the heap
Of bodies long since forsaken
Lost and lonely in their last sleep
So deep they'd never awaken

The politicians looked away
Blind to the truth so plain to see
They stole the lonesome souls that day
Of those statistics of society

Though the tongue finds the gnawing tooth
Of sleepers frozen in the sleet
Yet they feign to forget the truth
Of faceless figures on our streets

Daisy and Maggie and Dave died
Just so much stale meat on the street
Daisy and Maggie and Dave died
Three more statistics on our streets

The question that remains for us
So we know where each of us stands
Are they just our society's pus?
And their fate is sand in our hands?

Straight from the Horse's Mouth

Smack! Thwack! Whack!
Lash upon lash
Smack! Thwack! Whack!
Lash upon lash
The crack and the slash
The whip and the gash
Of course I'm just a horse
Screaming 'til I grew hoarse
Though I know in my gut what's true
So where are you now we need you, William Wilberforce?

I'm Jonjo Jacknori
Riding's my story, chasing glory
I grip the whip and just let rip
That's my job, that's my joy
In my hands she's my whipping-boy
Sometimes it's a matter of life and death
Sometimes she stings as she takes her last breath
Beating the bookie by beating the horse
That's no reason for our remorse
Rest assured
We don't give a monkey's about a whipped horse
When it comes to winning we're all whores

Train a foal for our goal
Add a callus to her heart and soul
That's our job, that's our joy

She then becomes our whipping-boy
We want our rookie to beat the bookie
We forget each lash as we count the cash
If she dies the prize is still in our eyes
If she loses when Jonjo uses too much force
That's no reason for our remorse
Rest assured
We don't give a monkey's about a whipped horse
When it comes to winning we're all whores

I'm here to place a bet
So I won't fret about her cold sweat
If she trips from too many flips
Dies from too many whips
Well when her life's last race is run
We'll just find another one for more fun
And end hers by a quick fire stun gun
That's our final choice for every horse
That's no reason for our remorse
Rest assured
We don't give a monkey's about a whipped horse
When it comes to winning we're all whores

I'm here to take the bets
I just don't care how hard the race gets
That's what it takes, those are the stakes
In our game there's some strife
It's just a horse losing her life
After all that's just the way the rain falls

Her pain and our gain are the twin limb calls
Sometimes an unlucky heart somehow stalls
That's no reason for our remorse
Rest assured
We don't give a monkey's about a whipped horse
When it comes to winning we're all whores

We're here to play to win
She's a running machine, not our kin
I've invested all my money
I'm here for the honey
Really don't care about the whip
When it's lashed across her hot hip and lip
You expect me to care about a horse?
That's a kind of nonsense I can't endorse
That's no reason for our remorse
Rest assured
We don't give a monkey's about a whipped horse
When it comes to winning we're all whores

We want to light our fuse
Though we know horses are born to lose
Sometimes we're a little too loud
We're the drunk party crowd
Our passion her dash on the bend
A swift blip from the whip and she'll soon mend
Then it's the stable or on the table
If she's a slacker straight to the knacker
That's no reason for our remorse

Rest assured
We don't give a monkey's about a whipped horse
When it comes to winning we're all whores

Smack! Thwack! Whack!
Lash upon lash
Smack! Thwack! Whack!
Lash upon lash
Thrash across my eyes
Hurt so I couldn't rise
Still screaming from my grave
A dead thoroughbred slave
Of course I'm just a horse
My Code a silent Morse
Caught under the jockey's thumbscrew
My tombstone tells a tale that's true
So where are you now we need you, William Wilberforce?

Blues for Harriet Tubman

Araminta Ross watched the burning cross
While her name flickered in the flame
When her Master sold her body
To Massa whose cruelty flowed through his veins
So she vowed to break the chains
Forged by law and stamped by birth
She broke them all and escaped on the run
To prove to the world her true worth

Up North she became Harriet Tubman
Risked her life in the Deep South
Saving slaves down in Maryland
Condemned to death from every Slavers' mouth
Each saved slave marked out her grave
A bounty placed on her head
Didn't stop her rescuing fugitives
Though the Slavers wanted her dead

Harriet beat them one and all
Living and fighting for freedom
Then died when she was 93
They placed her face on an American stamp
No longer cast as a runaway scamp
She became the face of black history

So can you measure the distance for me
It's so dark here I can hardly see
I'm blinded by the light of law and our history

Emmilene Pankhurst stepped beyond the law
When she hurled a cobbled stone
Through the Prime Minister's window
Sending the Suffragettes signed message home
They became State enemies
Force-fed women in prison
Pankhurst became one more human *foie gras*
To destroy her and her vision

Louise Hageby followed in the same vein
Her freedom fight fuelled by rage
She saw the plight of her sisters
The same as victims in a scientist's cage
They saw the law was used
In the cruel 'Brown Dog Affair'
They smashed the shambles of a science lab
To show the Government they cared

They fought the police in the streets
Then they torched the Gardens at Kew
Tube-fed by force they died and roared
Until the Government released them all
Freed from their cell they could enter the Hall
Then got what they fought for by a World War

So can you measure the distance for me
It's so dark here I can hardly see
I'm blinded by the light of law and our history

Ronnie Lee lived and worked in the law
For those facing a sentence
Serving the feckless and reckless
Seeking justice while they paid their penance
He aimed to support the weak
Their tongue often in a knot
Sometimes trying to prove their innocence
So they're not in a cell to rot

Then his sense of 'what is justice' shifted
When he saw the law was grim
Treating those who were different
Yet in many ways they were just like him
Looking in his cracked mirror
Figured they too should be free
As a lawyer he formed the A.L.F.
A beacon for their liberty

He changed and became a burglar
In his fight for their liberty
Saved the caged slaves in misery
Clad in black he burgled the basement lab
At night he became an underground Sab
Freeing our prisoners from agony

So can you measure the distance for me
It's so dark here I can hardly see
I'm blinded by the light of law and our history

I'm still not close enough to see
Who is blessed and who is cursed
Rescuing a slave in a field and one in a laboratory
Who is blessed and who is cursed
Rescuing a slave in prison and one in a laboratory
So help me unravel the laws bitter-sweet mystery
To see the difference between these three
Harriet and Louise and renegade Ronnie Lee

Statistics of Misery

Pump a pellet of poison through her
Jump her heart up to overload
Cast a chill for the cold-blooded kill
So her body starts to explode
Your answer to a cure for cancer
Always happens to be the same
Pick him as your next faceless victim
Just another number without a name

Millions and millions pile up in a stack
See the cash flow free from you and from me
Millions and millions pile up on the rack
See all our Statistics of Misery

Force-feed the dog one more overdose
Dressed to die he looks so depressed
Just one more pointless experiment
A truth the public won't have guessed
The scientist seeks another grant
To make the fat guinea-pig thin
Their violence concealed by their silence
While sad-eyed carcasses fill the trash bin

Fill the cat's tank with murky water
High enough to cover his eyes
As he tries to swim right to the brim
Only his corpse begins to rise
Funds that fill the professor's coffer
Injects every creature that moves
Kill the breeds for reports no one reads
A Degree in Suffering is all it proves.

Blind Faith/Blind Justice

Barrels of their blood and buckets of gore
Deep offal swill seeps under the door
Leave the stun gun 'cause you're in control
Cut out their hearts 'cause they've got no soul
The upturned cattle bleed over the floor
While greedy leaders plead for an encore
Shouting 'more, more, more' for profits galore
Hear the repertoire of your warm abattoir

Follow blind faith so they fail to see
Mock blind justice and make slaves of the free

You slaughter a creature you slaughter God
Fire the wire of the electric prod
While the chained cow writhes in the wired cage
Then slit her throat when she roars with rage
Then watch her drown slowly in bubbling blood
As her pain-stained face spurts a fountain flood
As you perform your ritual slaughter
A rite written in blood but writ in water

The new-born calf torn from her mother
Reminds Isaac of his long-lost mother
The calf sucks the slaughter man's fingers
The smell of her mother's fear lingers
All she drinks is the milk of human vice
His knife ends her life from his heart of ice

Calf and child cries through the eyes of Singer
Each mother forced through the gates of Treblinka

How we treat animals, the Nazi's treated us.
Are you on the side of the angels or Judas?

Bathsheba betrayed by one who bought her
Isaac knew her fate when they caught her
Nazis refused to give any quarter
Lined her up for their ritual slaughter
Memories of his mother's tattooed stamp
As Bathsheba was gassed in Herr Hitler's camp

Isaac Singer was a Jew
Who knew what was true
Saw ritual slaughter as a pale excuse
A dressed up disguise of animal abuse
Singer shot truth's arrow as the clincher
Catching the zealots hook, line and sinker:
To animals we are all Nazi's
And for them it's an eternal Treblinka

I Pity the Poseur Politician

I Pity the Poseur Politician
All their lives lined with lies
As they cast each false-hearted vote
So another animal dies
Their ears are deaf to truth and pain
When they fail to hear the last cries
Their ballot becomes a bullet
When another trapped badger dies

I Pity the Poseur Politician
Their tongues are tuned to lie
Finding their skewed kind of music
Blasting birds from a sour sky
They'll kill any creature that moves
A badger or fox or squirrel
Falsehoods float for the farmers' vote
If they're feral they're in peril

With an empty heart and a mind half-full
A vacant soul in a spirit so dull
What will be their next kill spins in their skull
They never count the cost of lives lost
Only the votes won in another cull

I Pity the Poseur Politician
For their eyes fail to see
Victims' blood spattered by the gun
As they face death without a plea
Without a reason to listen
As they find a tongue-tied scapegoat
They'll promise to revive hunting
So they gain one more tainted vote

An empty heart and a mind half-full
Matches their soul vacant and dull
Killing machines revolve in their skull
They never count the cost of lives lost
Only the votes won in another cull

The answer is stark like the dog that didn't bark
Capture those poseurs before they can bolt
Dispatch them with both barrels by the Pheasants'
Revolt

A Dog is just for Christmas

A Dog is just for Christmas
He'll amuse you with each caper
Then at the end of the day
Just chuck him away with the ripped wrapping paper

A Dog is just for Christmas
A living present for the day
Then when you're bored by her bark
Park in the dark and dump her on a motorway

A Dog is just for Christmas
A gift with a sense of sorrow
You can play with it all day
And decide to just toss it aside tomorrow

A Dog is just for Christmas
Much like the tinsel and the tree
Then when the day is over
You can just dump him with the rest of the debris

A Dog is just for Christmas
A rescued pooch the perfect pet
A gift you don't have to lift
Yet can sling him out without a trace of regret

A Dog is just for Christmas
Put another log on the fire
We'll have ashes to ashes
When you put another dog on the funeral pyre

A Dog is just for Christmas
Too good a taste to waste it's true
Stuff a mutt in the oven
To celebrate the Feast the way the Chinese do

A Dog is just for Christmas
A truth that's as pure as litmus
Roast the mutt with the turkey
Then we'll have the cutest quirky Chinese Christmas

Even Dogs who cannot read love this Poem

I was just seven when I visited book heaven after
reading about Doris being a bad dog
Because it was so much fun it made my head and heart
run like an unleashed dog
And after the tears and laughter rather than a quick jog
I raced all the way home
Then when I saw my Mum I breathlessly begged her
for a dog of my own

We rescued a 'rescue' dog who for me proved to be an
ideal match
As he was a bit scruffy with a piratical black eye I
called him Patch
From the start we went everywhere together as he
became my best friend
When we went to the Library he even helped to carry
the books I'd lend
Often at the Library I would catch Patch cast a glance
at me while I read
His eyes traced and tracked me as if he was echoing
the thoughts in my head

When I felt Patch was old enough I read to him all of
Doris's story
He listened intently to every word and seemed to
enjoy it as much as me
Although I know he is not the same breed as me he
still has a canine need

To learn the facts and share the fun books will feed
you and lead to
And as I have always thought a word is as potent as a
deed
Last Saturday night feeling the time was right I started
to teach Patch to read.

The Animal Rebellion Hellions

We are the Animal Rebellion
We are the new rage hellion
We are calling out animal abusers
We are here as your human accusers
We are the ghost of Animal Rebellion

We are the Animal Rebellion
We are the new rage hellion
We are the voice for those denied a human tongue
We are their voice to stop them being stung
We are the ghost of Animal Rebellion

We're here to free prisoners from your pens
We're here to protect and save all our penned friends

We are the Animal Rebellion
We are their hell-bent hellion
We are their planet battalion
We're wilder than a roped stallion
We're their genesis and your nemesis
We are the first and last Animal Rebellion

We are the Animal Rebellion
We are the new rage hellion
We'll show you what a band of men and women'll do
We're targeting all the criminals too
We are the ghost of Animal Rebellion

5

Morality and the Myth of Mortality

Historic scenes were witnessed at Tyburn by the crowd whose curiosity was aroused by the public spectacle and cruelty of a legal execution. A comparison can be drawn with this example where after the guilty verdict was delivered the defendant was taken to the gallows in the busy market square. As the crime was murder there was only one sentence: death. Before the hanging the defendant's face and legs were 'mangled and maimed'. That was an additional punishment and part of her sentence. The defendant's neck was stretched out and held by the hangman's assistant's rope. The noose was placed around her neck and tightened. She did not speak before she was killed; nor could she do so. She was mute merely by birth rather than malice. The defendant was an animal, a sow, executed after a trial as any ordinary common criminal. She was one more statistic of misery in our sordid legal history.

Her execution was captured as a frozen memory in a mural painted inside the local church. Although it was later removed the truth of the episode remains locked in time.

Whilst such rituals may seem a capricious relic of a bygone age in the 21st Century, the truth we must grasp is that animal trials happened throughout the world for more than 1000 years. Every kind of animal was ensnared by our ancestors in the legal net of time and crime. The proceedings were precisely the same as if a human was on trial with an indictment, a prosecution counsel, a defence counsel, a judge, a jury, evidence, witnesses and a verdict. When the defendant was convicted just like any human defendant the sentence would follow. Any animal would be subject to similar penal sentences ranging from exile to execution.

Animals were granted legal aid. If an animal was acquitted it would remain free to roam or be claimed by its owner. If convicted, an animal could appeal and the court could quash the conviction or amend the sentence. As with humans, for the animal criminal the trial was literally and legally a case of life and death.

The court presumed and placed animals on par with human criminals. Animals were bound by law. While that mural of the sow has vanished, the 'rights' imposed upon the animal criminals by law have vanished too.

Personifying animals as similar to humans meant accepting that they were rational beings. Then we could, as we did, hold them *personally* responsible for their actions. Their acts were voluntary and wilful against humans and in effect no different than the acts of ordinary criminals. All criminals deserved society's retribution. As animals were subject to the same laws, dangerous or destructive ones were bound to suffer the same fate as human miscreants and murderers. Animals were invested by us with reciprocal 'duties' and 'responsibilities' exactly like humans.

The logical result leads to a definite defined position: humans granted *legal rights* to animals. As we could not try them unless they possessed a 'legal personality', that is what happened. We imposed that status upon them so we could punish them as substitute humans. Animals were legally a reflection of our own imperfection. The trial was our attempt of a false justice in action. All it proved was that we subjected animals as ersatz humans to our own brand of injustice.

Animals were acting not as agents of God according to Aquinas, but 'the devil through them'. Therefore that is what the trials were 'aimed at' attempting to achieve. That theological explanation is typical of the lame excuses relied on by religious zealots as it tries to justify the culpability of animals. This self-serving defence is a one-sided pendulum where the church wins as the principle swings in their favour at the expense of the animal victim.

That is precisely why Beale J was so ahead of his time when in the classic American case, *Brown v. Eckes* [1850], involving the ownership of bees he said, 'Nothing is trivial that involves human rights.' The judge was nodding towards the fact that slavery was legal in America. He was confirming that the ownership of bees was feasible as a strand of the law. Equally he was noting that animal rights and human rights are linked.

Slavery is illegal in most of the modern world, yet animals remain categorised as chattels throughout the world. Animals are branded as our property because they have no value in their own right. While they are wild they are ownerless by our choice. When we breed or capture them we then deem them to be our property. We deem them to be inferior to us because, unlike us, we claim animals do not possess an immortal soul.

The belief is based on pure prejudice as it is to our advantage to practice such a bias. Animals are inferior by birth and they remain that way throughout their life and even on death. Notwithstanding our view on our soul, it is not merely immoral, it is suffused with falsehood. Consequently the fanciful idea should be foregone and the morality of treating animals properly be enshrined in a legal Charter. We can analyse the absurdity of our concept of the soul by examining these statements:

All animals are the only living beings born with an immortal soul.

All animals are denied from birth being blessed with an immortal soul.

All humans are the only living beings born with an immortal soul.

Those statements could be true or false according to history and religion and law and your own point of view. Who among us has a soul and who has not? Who can prove a self-serving proposition based purely on personal prejudice?

That is a question without an answer. Yet we have used it as a yardstick to give us a right to use animals for our own pleasure and purpose. Aristotle believed that slaves, women and animals were inferior to freemen. Perhaps it is obvious that he was a patrician. He considered that 'it is undeniably true that she [nature] has made all animals for the sake of man.' His bias was as natural as his self-proclaimed superiority. It was based on nothing less than prejudice. You cannot simply make a self-serving statement, assume that it is true and then use the assumption as a presumption that it is true. That is using a proposition as proof it is true. Instead of claiming that only humans have souls, there is no reason why we should not say that only animals have souls. Or we could extend that proposition to a tree or a pond or a cloud or any other item this side of cloud-cuckoo-land.

Where is the proof for such a perverse notion that 'humans alone have an immortal soul', any more than Aristotle's own? You can see how his ideas were formed by considering his view on the voiceless: 'The gift of speech also evidently proves that a man is a more social animal than the bees, or any of the herding cattle; for nature, as we say, does nothing in vain, and man is the only animal who enjoys it...'

If we denied those who are voiceless a legal voice in society then law would be deficient in its aim and purpose. There is not a doctor or a lawyer or a philosopher or a theologian on the planet that could prove that humans have a soul at all, immortal or otherwise. Moreover such a person could not prove that an animal did not have a soul. As a corollary such a person could not even begin to prove that while we are denied a soul, that condition is only shared by our fellow creatures rather than other humans. While the idea we have a soul while animals do not provides a cold comfort for our self-indulgent superiority, the notion falls far short of proof.

Only scientists such as Pereira and Descartes and ardent vivisectionists need to defend the indefensible and justify their injustice towards animals by the excuse that they lack a soul. There is not a person on the planet who could use a Cartesian creed or a philosophy or religion or theory to tender evidence that humans alone in the universe possess a soul. Moreover even if it were true it is so meaningless as to not matter one iota in respect of 'rights'. The late great visionary on the subject, Tom Regan, pinpointed the precise truth: 'Those who refuse to recognize the reasonableness of viewing many other animals, in addition to *Homo sapiens*, as having a mental life are the ones who are prejudiced, victims of human chauvinism – the conceit that we [humans] are *so* very special that we are the only conscious inhabitants on the face of the earth. The arguments and analysis of the present chapter sought to unmask this conceit.' Regan is right for one reason above all: our conceit is defeated by the manifest truth in our world.

Some lawyers and scientists are calling for robots to be granted a 'legal personality'. In 2017 the European Parliament took a step towards identifying robots as 'electronic persons'. The present progress on the subject presents the blatant truth that our bias places artificial intelligence above an animal's consciousness: it measures morality by using a mirror which reflects our natural prejudice making animals of less value than a robot.

That is proof we are infecting ourselves with the contagious disease of conceit.

6

An A-Z of Immorality

All the talking in the world, whether it is an academic ivory tower or at a palatial festival gathering or a convention, is as useful as a drunken discourse on Descartes in the local pub. There is a tendency for the talkers to do just that: talk and talk and talk so their vast egos walk. It is of little value to the speaker and of no value at all to the listener. This A-Z is an outline of our outliers namely all animals. It sets out the position we place animals in within our society and proves why their status must be changed by law. That is essential on two mercenary levels namely to save them from us and from our own perpetual folly.

The emphasis is on deeds, not words. Their plight and the future of animal rights, both starts and ends with the law. This A-Z is a prelude to the shape of a future Animals' Charter.

We have still to learn the lesson delivered by Ruth Harrison in *Animal Machines* [1964] where she flayed the growing practice of factory farming. The book was so startling in form and stunning in its conclusion it led to a public outcry which forced the government to act. That led to new legislation being introduced. Half a century later Harrison's raw truth remains live: 'that *the animals do not live before they die*, they only exist.'

For self-serving reasons we are unwilling to reach for let alone grasp the granite truth of Mary Midgley: 'We are not just like animals; we *are* animals.'

These A-Z Notes are an outline of our present legal position regarding the status of animals. They provide a reason why that position has always been the case and remains unacceptable. Words are better than bullets as they only kill with kindness. Deeds that tender protection to those that need it are the best of all. Better then to not only aim for the right target, but make sure you hit it too. All other aspects affecting animals' lives pale into insignificance against a legal right to exist. The only effective ammunition we can use is the law.

Advocate:

The time for a legal representative to be appointed to protect animals within our society is long overdue. Unlike every other body within our society that is disadvantaged on grounds of age, disability, ethnicity, gender, race, sex or otherwise, animals alone have no such legal representation.

Animals need an Advocate for precisely the same reason that those persons who are equally unequal and under the act or threat of discrimination need one.

Their need is if anything so much greater because they have no means of dissent or objection.

For animals to have a future in our society they need rights with a human face. Essentially they need what we have: a legal representative, an Animals' Advocate. Animals need a legal representative for precisely the same reason: to counteract discrimination. An Advocate should be appointed with these powers and responsibility namely to:

1. Promote and protect the rights and interests of all animals, domestic and wild.

2. Initiate court proceedings on their behalf when necessary.

3. Represent animals in Court where any action affects their rights and future.

4. Represent animals in Parliament where any Bill affects their rights and future.

5. Liaise with the Law Commission to introduce a new Animal Rights Act.

6. Introduce the paramount principle of granting animals a legal personality.

7. Provide Annual Reports which are disclosed direct to the public.

8. Invite applications from the public as to reporting of any form of animal abuse.

9. Be independent of any political party.

10. Be independent of any other non-political or social organisation.

11. Be accountable to the High Court as opposed to Parliament.

12. Allow and be subject to Judicial Review by any member of the public.

Of course everything sounds revolutionary when it is either new or against the existing order of matters or is somehow unsettling to those who have a present advantage over others. It follows that all the features advanced that tender an advantage to the others who are affected are opposed by those who bear the loss. That applies equally to animals and us.

The Magna Carta [1215] states: 'to no one will we sell, to no one will we deny or delay right or justice'. With an Advocate being appointed the 'one' is not limited to humans. That is as it should be.

The clarion call of the slave masters and traders in opposing abolition of slavery was, 'who will pick my cotton? What will happen to our economy? Why should these people be free? Why should we free them? After all are we not their masters?'

Angling:

Angling should become illegal. It seems stark to write and read that statement as it applies to what some people perceive and even believe is a 'sport'. It might be but only from the side of the one making the killing. Indeed, to save repetition on every aspect of this A-Z category, that statement of declaring all such animal abuse 'should become illegal', equally applies to every form of that treatment by us.

The statement will not be repeated in detail when considering it from an animal's position as it is plain beyond dispute. The conclusion follows the premise in a logical furrow towards each life being recognised by law.

Yet the realistic position, regardless of the constant stream of excuse-after-excuse from anglers that fish are 'cold-blooded' creatures, is fish do feel pain and undergo suffering when hooked from the water. All the evidence proves that position. It is surely elementary that to hook a fish and drag it from the water and then, with a damaged mouth and all that that entails for the creature's future, throw it back into the water, causes the fish to suffer. How could it be otherwise? Do they say they have never heard a fish scream? Could anglers choose a better angle by perhaps experimenting on themselves?

If it is for their table to share a biblical-style meal with the loaves, it is still unacceptable. When someone is suffering from starvation is a separate matter. Nevertheless except in such extreme circumstances, what gives us the right to deprive an animal of their life, especially so just to satisfy a palate?

Anglers know the truth. That is why they rely on the false claim that fish are cold-blooded creatures when in truth the only cold-blooded creatures are those holding the rod and hook.

A more realistic appraisal was coined by Byron about Walton who boasted of how he found fishing to be such a wonderful sport: 'The quaint, old, cruel coxcomb, in his gullet should have a hook, and a small trout to pull it.'

Angling is our literal form of shooting fish in a barrel. They have no means of escape which adds to our pleasure and their demise. Angling is the obverse side of the same counterfeit coin that is a circus. Each only serves our purpose of showing us that animals are mere commodities. They are not our playthings nor should they be classified as our property. All that classification entails is legal subservience and abuse.

For animals, looking out from the inside, whether it is an abattoir or a cage or a river or the sky, our world is a sad spectacle mixed-up of a circus and a zoo. All of it is designed to cause them legal suffering.

Of course it is a conspiracy that is so much better for us. Together we conspire to make a dog's dinner of their position for we own the dog and the dinner. The advantage we possess is we can collectively shelve our consciences and forget as a matter of morality, echoed by law, that one woman's lunch is another animal's life.

Bail:

Rather than be kept in a cage for months and sometimes years while the case drags on through the courts, animals should have a right to bail. When they are kept in custody it affects their mental disposition. The result is an abused animal is further abused by the legal system.

If a rapist can get bail, an animal is at least more deserving than that member of our species.

A dog deemed to be 'dangerous', might be there for years. Irwin J in the *Housego Case* [2012] noted the aftermath of an allegation that is often overlooked: 'After this dog has been kept on death row, so to speak, for more than two-and-half years, it is time she was reprieved.'

The dog was then set free. How she was affected by the incarceration remains unknown.

Once a dog has been deemed to be 'dangerous', it can be colloquial as well as legal that you 'give a dog a bad name' which then determines their fate. In the Canadian High Court case of *R v Houdek* [2008] Smith J considered the aim and approach the court should adopt.

The judge quashed a destruction order and concluded: 'In determining whether a dog is dangerous, the assessment must be in the context of a dog acting in the normal way of canines. When dealing with an analysis which may lead to a finding of a dog being declared dangerous, the quality of mercy should not be strained.'

The allusion to 'the quality of mercy' is particularly pertinent given that Shakespeare's play where it appears, *The Merchant of Venice*, examines prejudice in a court case. While that reference applies to Jews, our treatment of them resembles the connection between racism and speciesism simply because it accurately reflects that connection.

These cases show the courts were concerned about the effect of the process on those dogs. A 'fair' trial for living creatures takes into account that an unfair trial could result in their death. Moreover you could only show 'mercy' to one who is sentient.

The law barely takes account of that at all. Only in extreme cases is such sentience even recognised. It should be the norm as animals suffer because they can feel pain.

Hence bail should follow unless, as with a human, there is some valid reason to keep the defendant or the dog in custody.

Bee:

Aristotle had misguided ideas about bees. Those ideas were mainly overlooked because of his supposed brilliance. He was closer to the 'Naked Emperor' as he believed bees did not copulate and drones do not participate in generation. He even criticised bees as being incapable of feeling because they could not speak. His reputation allowed him to rely on nonsense and dress it up as 'philosophy'. As with many of his ideas it was cod philosophy.

Given that conclusion, it is little wonder that other so-called 'scientists' such as Pereira and Descartes and Pavlov followed in his hollow footsteps. Using the Aristotelian approach served to allow them and us to treat animals unfairly and unjustly. It was worse in that Aristotle enabled us to conceive a solipsistic idea that we are superior to all other animals on the planet. Such self-serving falsehood has fed our ego ever since. In turn we intubate that notion as a legal tenet.

The position of bees says it all: they could do without us, yet we would perish without them. Therefore our present action in killing them with pesticides is pure folly. We do so because it generates short-term profits as well as using our power over bees.

Cattle:

Scientists are now working on a way to produce cattle

that will fatten quickly, but will eat less. That has a distinct advantage for us as it leads to more profits and less methane. For the methane is helping to destroy our environment and planet. Ultimately it means we will produce specially designed cows that will have a lower level of flatulence.

The scientists are presently scrambling to produce cows that will not fart as much as they do now. Perhaps they could then turn to the ever-present problem of being trapped in a lift with a silently effluvium expelling man by producing a perfumed fart.

Yet there is a distinct tendency to be sceptical of the reasons for these advances and perhaps smell a rat. For they always seem to result in more cows in less space and fatter gains for the shareholders.

Charter:

Regardless of the reason for introducing the Magna Carta, the spirit it imbues is what matters. We still invoke that spirit over 800 years later. It is why when Radhakrishnan J in the Indian Supreme Court considered the cultural custom of Jallikattu, a 'bull-running' episode where animals are treated without thought or mercy as goods to be abused for their pure amusement. In the *Animal Welfare Board Case* [2014] he delivered a bellwether judgment:

Legal rights shall not be the exclusive preserve of the humans which has to be extended beyond people thereby dismantling the thick legal wall with humans all on one side and all non-human animals on the other side...animals are denied rights, an anachronism which must necessarily change.

Although the event was entered into by the complete community including the police for centuries, Radhakrishnan J ruled the custom was sadistic and declared it illegal.

In the *NOAH Case* [2003] the Supreme Court of Israel had to rule whether force-feeding geese was cruel. It is a practice analogous to that used on suffragettes in prison with fatal consequences. Rivlin J delivered a perceptive judgment:

As for myself, there is no doubt in my heart that wild creatures, like pets, have emotions. They were endowed with a soul that experiences the emotions of joy and sorrow, happiness and grief, affection and fear. No one denies that these creatures also feel the pain inflicted upon them through physical harm or a violent intrusion into their bodies... acts of artificial force-feeding, justification whose essence is the need to retain the farmer's source of livelihood and enhance the gastronomic delight of others...But this has a price – and the price is reducing the dignity of Man himself.

He ruled the practice was cruel. It was abolished in 2005. The impact of that case was such that it shut down the *foie gras* industry in Israel.

It is reminiscent of a similar force-feeding practice that was used on recalcitrant suffragettes in prison with dire consequences for their health: all women suffered, some even died. The connection is that at that time women had little or no power to resist such blatant injustice. Their position then remains the same for animals now.

A practice that delights a palate while causing suffering to animals is patently an abuse. The same approach applies to any ritual based on custom or religion that causes suffering. Whether it relates to a palate or a prayer the practice should be illegal.

Those judgments should be compared to our own judges who in the then highest court in the country, the House of Lords, in the *National Anti-vivisection Society Case* [1948] declared:

> The scientist who inflicts pain in the course of vivisection is fulfilling a moral duty to mankind which is higher in degree than the moralist or sentimentalist who thinks only of the animals. Nor do I agree that animals ought not be sacrificed to man when necessary ...There is only one single issue.

Is there 'only one single issue'? Is it 'a moral duty to mankind' to consider animals you control are morally and legally inferior to you? Or is it pure prejudice? Is that merely the perverse Aristotelian philosophy in action? Is it simply Descartes revisited? Is it proof that our legal system is unfit for purpose in protecting animals from us?

Whichever way it is spliced the result is the same: we do it because our might makes it right.

Such a notion underlines the value of speciesism within our legal process. Equally it undermines the value of animals as living creatures. That above all is one reason why we need An Animals' Charter.

Circus:

In 2019 a bear 'mauled' his Russian trainer in the ring. Why should that result shock us? What could be more natural for any confined creature than to kick against the pricks? That was the thought and term that lit in St Peter's mind when he too was persecuted. Animals compelled to prance around in an unnatural environment and engage in practised tricks for our amusement is both never right and always a wrong against the victim.

Circuses are well beyond their time because morally their time never existed at all. Parading animals around a sawdust ring as a form of our community fun is indefensible. In every form they should be abolished if they rely on animals to provide a money-making machine.

Circuses are a way for us to increase profits and amuse those who are easily amused providing it is at someone else's expense. Well as for Juvenal's critical satirical comment that the denizens only want 'bread and circuses', let them have bread, if necessary, and drizzle cake too. As for circuses perhaps the ringmaster could become the back end of a pantomime horse. Why not put the ringmaster in the stocks where we could have a revived community fun by mocking him? Or better still, wear a top hat and crack a whip?

A circus explains the atavistic appeal of the Elephant-Man-syndrome as it purveys prejudice as a playful parade. It panders to our bullying bias of those unable to resist. At the bottom of a convenient pliable pile are animals. It is why Radhakrishnan J said:

Animal Welfare Act of 2006 (U.K.) also confers considerable protection to the animals from pain and suffering...

Rights and freedoms guaranteed to the animals under [the Indian Animal Welfare Act] have to be read along with...the Constitution, which is the magna carta of animal rights.

It is salient that that Indian Act is superior in protecting animals as compared to English law. It is doubly ironic that the judge compares the content to the Magna Carta. That is why we now need An Animals' Charter.

Clones:

From Dolly the cloned sheep onwards, clones prove animals are mere commodities to be bred as our experimental creatures. It is a modern phenomenon that echoes the experiments of Mengele at Auschwitz. He started with animal mutilation. Of course he swiftly moved from animals to Jews because he had power over his exhibits. It is the usual way and yet another reason why it is immoral and should be illegal.

Meanwhile the biologist Nakauchi and his team are trying to target their own treatment of animals to detect the percentage of rodent brains that are human. If it exceeds 30 they will suspend the experiment. These are part of the government's conditions to prevent a 'humanised' animal from ever coming into existence. Nakauchi and his team at Stanford successfully made the first human-sheep embryo in 2018 which was destroyed after 28 days. It had very few human cells. His humanity was confirmed by his pronouncement that 'we are trying to ensure that the human cells contribute only to the generation of certain organs.' Fortunately Nakauchi had covered any potential objection to his experiments as they 'targeted organ generation' which meant they avoided 'human cells integrating where we don't want them.' What is especially important to him and his team is that as a result 'there should be many fewer ethical concerns.' Well that is alright then. It is gratifying to know that in these experiments they are only sacrificing animals. Even better is the fact that Nakauchi is untroubled by too many 'ethical concerns.'

With time we will be able to climb the animal-human ladder of clones where robots are all but our blood-brothers. When science progresses up that ladder, will the result be part-rodent/part-robot and if so, depending on the percentage of the part-human too, how will the exhibit be classed as a matter of law? Further, given that the inherent prejudice of the scientist is now feared to be transmitted to the robot, will the new exhibit be biased in favour of the scientist-inventor or against his animal and human victims or a mixture of all those features?

Given that drug dealers can easily train their trophy dogs to hate and attack their enemies, be they other gang members or the police, it opens up the opportunity for discrimination. Whether it is witting or unwitting is not the point, but the fact it is feasible. That is the feature that should concern us.

Nevertheless it is an embryonic time-bomb silently ticking away to one day present a legal problem, if instead of being wholly a different species, the creature contains human feelings and failings as well as a genetic make-up. When is an animal an animal and when is a human a human if the scientific opened door is Einstein meets Frankenstein? Perhaps we could use vivisection to prove our superiority?

Court:

The courts must be vigilant to identify animal abuse and treat abusers in a way that reflects the gravity of the offence. At present and for the past few centuries since 'cruelty' to animals became an offence they have consistently treated offenders with undue leniency. Part of the problem is that such abuse has never been and is not taken seriously by judges. Another aspect is that often there is little difference between the offender and the court. That is not a reflection on the character of the magistrate, but the inherent bias of our society and legal system.

Allied to that we have had a series of politicians claim they wished to revive fox hunting. Yet the politicians' promise and notion is one that filters through our legal system and infects how abusers are treated. That should be considered in relation to the myth as compared to the truth of what the supposed blood sport actually involves. The leniency with which animal abusers are treated stems from the legislation which limits the sentence so most cases are heard in the lower courts, the Magistrates' Court. Consequently the sentence remains low too. The maximum sentence of six months' imprisonment reflects the fact that animal abuse is of no consequence. The proposed increase to a maximum of 5 years' imprisonment remains inadequate.

Cull

Culls are always borne of economics. However we dress it up it still comes down to money.

We introduce an animal and then when that breed becomes too many we decide we would prefer to kill them all. We may have the social excuse of calling them 'pests' or 'vermin', but the real reason is we do it because we can get away with it.

Who can object? Whether it is a badger or a squirrel they all exist at their peril if they cause us any loss of income. Today it is the grey squirrel. Tomorrow we will find fault with the red squirrel. We view animals as the Chinese see the pangolin.

It really does not matter whether it is a beaver or a stoat, we will kill them if it excites us on any spurious ground. Our real aim is shown by our favoured result: dodo justice.

Brian May, a guitarist with a popular combo, was castigated for using the word genocide to refer to animals. As a result he somewhat sheepishly apologised and explained his reason for using the term. He was wrong to apologise as he was right to use such a term. What word could be more exact to describe our aim and approach in treating animals as goods to use for our own purpose from birth to death? Is it not similar to holocaust which similarly applies to animals for the same reason? Given the etymology of 'holocaust' relates to animal sacrifice, why should we shrink from the truth?

In a twist that only a tyrant could turn to his advantage, in 1976 Marcos expelled the complete Calauit community of 254 indigenous people and replaced them with imported African animals. It was his personal private zoo. The families he expelled were naturally deprived of their rights. They counted for nothing because they were 'only people'. Marcos saw them as being of less value than the antelopes and zebras he imported. Moreover who cared what happened to stateless people without a legal voice?

The Calauit were only a mirror-image of what we see when we reflect on our vision of animals that then determines our decision, much the same way they were viewed by Marcos.

We have the same scenario in our history of introducing pine martens so they can kill squirrels. In time they will be perceived by us as a problem and we will have another cull.

Descartes:

Descartes was so misguided and cursed with a warped mind he had a pregnant cow killed so he could examine her foetus.

However we should not be shocked let alone surprised by that act. For Descartes was responsible, directly and indirectly, for the abuse and torture of millions of animals over the centuries. His crass ideas that animals were *automatons* proved his lack of compassion and intellect. Then again he was a liar too. Indeed he knew he was dishonest in his view as he later admitted he was indulgent to people as it absolved them from 'any suspicion of crime, however often they may eat or kill animals.'

Even before his captious confession, Voltaire identified Descartes as a mere 'machinist' which was an accurate though excoriating insult.

Professor Henry Holzer identified the unassailable truth about him:

> As influential as was Aquinas, the philosophical father of animal abuse was probably the renowned philosopher-mathematician Rene Descartes. Animals, he held, were automatons – literally. Therefore, he asserted, animals experienced neither pleasure nor pain. Doubtless, this theory provided Descartes with the rationalization necessary to allow his dissection of unanesthetized animals.

In practice it was a human conspiracy borne of self-interest and confirmed by our ancestors' silence. At heart Descartes was part scientist and part politician and part quack plus wholly a charlatan.

Yet at its worst our law has a Cartesian strain that reflects our assessment of animals as things to be abused and consumed and killed. That is a mirror-image of Descartes' philosophy.

Dog Racing

Dog racing should become illegal. Dogs are compelled to run fast as a money-making machine. When they are too old or unfit or just past their prime, they are cast aside as naturally and wantonly as Christmas wrapping paper on Boxing Day. A greyhound that does not make money for the owner and punter and stadium boss has no value. For the main part it is a view shared by society in a shroud of apathy and silence.

Horse racing is the same for the same reason. The social spectacle and money that is generated is a ready-made reason to overlook the abuse of the animals. It is indeed the sport of kings in using horses as things. Things we pamper and train to run and jump over high fences and then routinely kill if they are injured. They start as running machines and end as malfunctioned machines.

Any sport that employs animals as property to be used for our gain and their pain should be illegal. There is no reason to do so save for the fact we can get away with it because no one objects on their behalf. Our amusement at dogs racing to catch a furry rabbit is a prime example of why they and we need an Advocate.

Boxing, whether you are for or against it as a 'sport', is quite different. There two people legally assault each other for a vast financial purse. They do so by consent and willingly risk their own lives. It is a commercial proposition where their gain and pain is related to their choice and decision. Hence it is the direct opposite of all sports where we use animals. Then they take the risk and we take the money.

Eating:

We deny animals some food we grow so we can use it to feed other animals that we can kill and then use those animals as our food. It is an endless chain of mass induced misery.

It is not a question of compelling people to eat grass or seaweed. There is no escape from the fact, however unpalatable it is for us to face and grasp, that every time we eat an animal we are depriving a living creature of their life. Moreover we can quite easily survive, let alone exist, without the need to eat animals. The fact that we do eat them is a result of our conspiracy as the benefit to all humans is that animals have no legal means of resisting us. Our selfish desires are shared by other humans. Therefore why should we change at all?

We could always adopt the Swiftian idea that we eat the children of the poor. Although a balance may be achieved and in terms of diet could be preferable, by adopting Wells idea of eating the rich. An unexpected bonus would be to help solve our current crisis of obesity too. That could lead to the best of all worlds. Who would object as those likely to would already be dead? The objection would be that humans are somehow special, are homo sapiens, have a soul, are superior to animals which we own. That belief is the base and core of our superiority. As they are inferior their suffering is ignored and lack of status validates speciesism. Compared to the ever-expanding obesity crisis that threatens the demise of the NHS, surely it is valid to consider eating the poor and the rich?

Often people who eat animals languidly declare, 'I feel sorry for the animals, but, well, I like meat', as if that is the only relevant point. When you hear such comments your thoughts stray to an unspoken answer, 'well, maybe like you they would like to live too'. As it is easier to eat meat than show compassion, our diet and digestion must be subject to law. Otherwise a satisfied palate is merely another ritual, no different in its own way than a religious one. There is no compromise: an animal must be protected from our call on their bodies by law.

Our relationship with animals was considered in *R. v. Menard* [1978] by the Quebec Court of Appeal where Lamer JA said:

It does not mean that man, when a thing is susceptible of causing pain to an animal, must abstain unless it is necessary but means that man in the pursuit of his purposes as a superior being, in the pursuit of his well-being, is obliged not to inflict on animals pain, suffering or injury which is not inevitable taking into account the purpose sought and the circumstances of the particular case. In effect, even if it is not necessary for man to eat meat if he could abstain from doing so, as many in fact do, it is the privilege of man to eat it.

Lamer JA candidly claimed that any rules made are purely in the 'interests of man'. Consistent with that concept he explained our self-importance and 'privilege' to 'eat it'. Whatever might be our self-importance, it must be balanced by an animal's claim to life. Much like other aspects of our treatment of animals, we must change our diet and philosophy.

Films:

Passages in films that openly portray animal abuse as gratuitous violence with no point or purpose except to massage salacious minds should become illegal.

That is the same reason that pornography and 'snuff movies' are popular within the murky minds of paedophiles and similar warped characters. Indeed it is why it makes money for the pornographers. All of it, particularly the manner of Lynch and Tarantino to slip in a brief dog fighting incident in passing, underscores the perversion. Equally it undermines their claim it is just 'entertainment'. It is discrimination of an inferior animal by taking advantage of their inferiority just because you can do so. That is the reason and the rhyme behind the discrimination. It is also the reason that black people are used to abuse animals as pornographic pawns. Together it combines the allure of racism and sexism and speciesism. More than all of that, the main reason it remains is it makes money for the film makers.

Five Freedoms:

The Animal Welfare Act 2006 relies on the term 'welfare' to protect animals. By relying on welfare it was positively and purposely using a term that was usually applied to children. That concept of welfare was endorsed by the Farm Animal Welfare Council which concluded that all animals should have the Five Freedoms which are:

1. Freedom from hunger and thirst.

2. Freedom from discomfort.

3. Freedom from pain, injury and disease.

4. Freedom to express normal behaviour.

5. Freedom from fear and distress.

It is now far too tame in form and factors as the many changes in farming since it was proposed in 1965. Then agriculture did not have factory-farming on the scale that now exists which will only grow exponentially and inexorably in the future. The Five Freedoms are no longer fit for purpose. They should be amplified and extended to every situation that relates to animals, domestic and wild, that we subject to as our victims.

It is sutured into our society so the past and present will in turn become their future. That time has now passed. For it looks to a few ideas that will ensure animals are fed and watered. Food and water may placate our delicate minds, but it does little to protect the victims. You might as well give a modern day slave free condoms so she is not impregnated as that will affect her value to the trader. The Five Freedoms are sterile and stale and for another place and time. A Future Freedom should replace it with a guarantee that the recipient animal has a future which recognises their value and assesses their worth as important to them.

There is one quintessential difference in what each signifies for the holder: The future is not to promote their welfare, but their rights. Welfare refers to their care, rights guarantees a life.

When they were introduced the Five Freedoms were hailed as being progressive. Thereafter they have been followed as a code and guideline throughout the world. Yet even where they have been noted, the result was not overlooked by the judge. However Radhakrishnan J wisely went much farther by stating:

> The guidelines of World Health Organization of Animal Health recognizes five internationally recognized freedoms for animals...Rights and freedoms guaranteed to the animals under ...the Indian Animal Welfare Act have to be read along

with ...the Constitution, which is the magna carta of animal rights.

Fur:

People who wear fur only prove they are naturally obtuse. It is not a question of wearing the coat that an animal has been tortured to death so that you can indulge your vanity, though in some way that would be enough of an objection. The real objection is their caveman mentality shows their mind is ugly on the outside too.

In 2019 California became the first American State to 'ban animal fur products'. It is proposed to become law in 2023. Peta [People for the Ethical Treatment of Animals] claimed, 'Today is a historic day for animals in California'. Conversely the Fur Information Council claims the fur trade is worth about $1.5 billion to the American economy. They fear that it is part of a 'radical vegan agenda using fur as the first step to other bans on what we wear and eat.'

Well the answer to that is what is wrong about banning omnivorous cannibalism and slavish fashion vanity purely because it is another species? Moreover why wait four years to introduce the new law? Why was it not now? Or better still, why was it not introduced yesterday or yester-year?

Grebe:

Women driven by fashion figured that the feathers which birds were born with would enhance their beauty. As a result their feathers were plucked and placed in their quirky hats. The calculated consequence was that certain birds almost became extinct. Among them was the grebe.

You can see on this book's cover that the feathers look better on the bird. The cover illustrates why animals need our loud voice to be their legal voice. We are exhorted not to 'judge a book by it's cover'. Here you can do so because the message is true. The grebe was in danger in the past from feather-wearing-fashionists just as it is a potential victim of decoy clowns who think shooting a bird at close range is a fine form of fun.

The hooded grebes have become a critically endangered species, with only about 1,000 individuals remaining in the wild. About 20 different species make up the grebe family. Long-term declines were noted between the 1960s and 1990s in many parts of its range due to loss of wetland habitat and residual effects from exposure to DDT and other pesticides. The pied-billed grebe is considered endangered or threatened particularly in the north eastern states of America.

It is dodo justice in action where we cull and destroy and kill animals for some superficial reason. The dodo chimes with injustice as we hunted them to extinction because we could.

Horse Racing:

Horse racing should become illegal. Horses are whipped to make them run faster. They are made to jump fences that are dangerous. Horses regularly die in the process year-on-year. One dead horse is one too many. That is accentuated by the fact the supposed 'sport' is supported by money so the horses are just a financial means to their grubby end.

In several countries the use of a whip is illegal. It is legal in England, but should be banned by law as should horse racing itself. Though there are multiple vested interests in making money from horses being seen as running machines, there is an unanswered question: if they wish to run, as is claimed by everyone who uses one, why whip a horse at all?

Hunting:

Let us move away from the pretty postcard image of red coated jolly men and women on horseback supping a glass of chilled wine with the village peasants before wandering into the countryside to engage in destroying a few pests and assorted vermin. That is stereotypical and as stale as a Grimm story or Robin Hood revisited. All the excuses cannot hide the truth decay that rots the false image the hunters portray.

Rather than consider the points for and against the hunting of wild animals for fun, it is more instructive to consider actual cases. That is advantageous as it tells the truth about the pursuit which is based on evidence not opinion. Hence it is of value to consider the truth from the hunter's own tongue:

Shooting and gassing foxes does not create that 'sporting' chance...although hunting people would not want me to put it quite like this, in an increasingly humdrum world, fox hunting also preserves a great eccentric tradition in the countryside.

This 'great eccentric tradition' is a euphemism for sadism. That is the reason for making such an activity illegal. The history and spectacle are different lies of the same counterfeit coin. The truth is written in the screams of the captive foxes as they meet their death.

Hybrid:

From Dolly onwards it is more than mere scientific curiosity. It is borne of and based on the economics of misery. For the victims that is as useful as compared to the entrepreneurs and scientists. What happens to all the hybrids? What are they classed as in the scheme of species?

The stem cell biologist Nakauchi has been waiting for this moment for more than a decade. After years of planning, the persistent researcher has at last received approval from a government willing to pursue one of the most controversial scientific studies there is: human-animal embryo experiments.

Why was 'approval' given? Where will it end? Isaac Bashevis Singer was accurate and on target in his assessment that 'in relation to them we are all Nazi's: for the animals it is an eternal Treblinka.'

Isonomy:

Isonomy guarantees the principle of equality for everyone subject to law. That principle cannot be used to abuse or exclude anyone.

That concept is loosely contained within the aim of the Animal Welfare Act 2006 and the Dangerous Dogs Act 1991 as amended. Each Act attempts to control us in our treatment of animals as otherwise we can harm other people and them. Regardless of whether our acts are intentional or reckless the result is the same. Yet both are flawed laws in origin and action. For in practice each Act fails to grant protection to an animal's right to live. It is another reason why we need an Animal Rights Act.

Justice:

Justice is concerned with 'levelling' or treatment of others, be they of the same or a different species. It is the heart and mind and soul of a valid legal system. For a legal system that has that spirit pervading its sinews promotes equal treatment for those subject to it. At present at its best that applies to people. To be the best it must also apply to animals. A legal system that fails to recognise the rights of animals thereby concurs in purveying injustice.

The potential discrimination of dogs within the judicial system was considered in the High Court in such circumstances. In *Knightsbridge Crown Court Case* [1996] Elsa had been sentenced to death and her owner could not afford the fees which might have freed her. On appeal Lord Justice McCowan [LJ] addressed the issue head-on and delivered a positive description of what the trial process should achieve:

> I would not criticise the Commissioner for making the application, it is important, in my judgment, that if the application were to be made, no steps should be taken which would prevent the dog having a fair trial. The relevant facts were that the applicant had no legal aid, no right of appeal to the Crown Court and no means to pay the £300...by insisting on a figure of £300 contribution to be made by the Applicant, the Commissioner made it well near impossible for the Applicant to get a fair trial for his dog.

McCowan LJ concluded, 'there was not, in the result, a fair trial.' The court quashed the destruction order on Elsa and ordered a rehearing.

The other judge in that appeal, Collins J, emphasised what must be the aim of the court conducting the rehearing:

It seems to me that it is all the more important that the Magistrate, before whom the matter comes, ensures that there is a fair trial.

In *Housego Case* [2012] the High Court has shown a prescience regarding the sentience of an incarcerated dog. The time between an alleged offence being committed and a trial and subsequent appeal is often lengthy, certainly months and maybe some years. Irwin J noted the effect and took immediate action:

After this dog has been kept on death row, so to speak, for more than two-and-half years, it is time she was reprieved.

These cases show the courts were concerned about the effect of the process on those dogs. Unusually the judges took their feelings into account.

Killing:

It may be true as Paul Simon sings that there are '50 ways to leave your Lover'. However there are many more than 50 ways to kill an animal. Moreover, if there is a way to do so, rest assured we will stumble upon the method. Where our pleasure is concerned, their pain is secondary. For animals humans are in aim, approach, aspiration and attainment a mass mechanical killing machine. It is manifestly true that Black Lives Matter. Nevertheless, though there is a defined connection between racism and sexism and speciesism, as a matter of law animals' lives do not matter. In that respect the law accurately represents us.

Language:

'Animals' is a term of abuse often used by humans to describe violent football fans and drunken thugs who run amok during demonstrations that were planned to be peaceful. 'Animals' as a pejorative term has become so widespread it was used in 2016 to describe a convicted paedophile who had slyly groomed and coy-duck style indecently assaulted a child. However, notwithstanding the history of our universal practice of putting animals on trial as common criminals for over 1000 years, it is humans who commit crimes against other humans and animals. Few, if any, violent crapulent animal criminals invade a football pitch when their team is losing or hunt humans to death for fun. In 2016 a purblind American politician with a suicide-dyed toupee branded protesting arsonists as 'animals'.

Using words to describe animals to describe people is discriminatory and a hate crime. Although it is not a specified offence, it should be because 'bitch' and 'cow' and 'dog' to describe women is plainly prejudicial. Such words are often used by racists and rapists to justify their actions and conduct.

Legislation:

When we consider 'welfare' as a concept, we are generally dealing with someone who is vulnerable and in need of assistance lest they are exploited by other less scrupulous individuals. The vulnerability is respected and accounted for within our social services. Usually it is children or adults who are disabled or those in need of food banks or shelter. Conversely where animals are concerned we have no representative save for indirectly by some lacklustre government departments and worthy charities.

Welfare is of limited value to animals as it merely means that they are more links in their chains. So they can move a bit better while we anchor their ball to a human tether.

All the numerous different statutes that monitor our movements regarding our domestic creatures such as bees and cats and dogs and wildlife of every form are negative. They are predicated upon the idea that animals are our property. Our legal position then advances a position which ostensibly is to protect the particular animal, but actually protects us and our use of property or ownership when we acquire a wild one.

We grant a limited protection to dogs so we can punish the owner and kill the dog if one bites a human. Who represents the 'defendant' dog?

The legislation that affects all animals whether they are

domestic or wild, within or outside our society, rests on animals being our legal property. That specific reason is what is wrong about our law. As a corollary it is why we need to sweep away all the present legislation that governs our treatment of animals.

An amendment is quite straightforward as a matter of law as can be seen by the 'new' Act, Animal Welfare (Service Animals) Act 2019 which originated as a Private Member's Bill. It provides an additional protection for police dogs and horses while being used by a constable.

That is a small step. It is nowhere near enough. What is needed is all the present legislation must be repealed and replaced by a composite statute namely the Animal Rights Act 2020.

Morality:

Nietzsche claimed that 'morality is the herd-instinct in the individual.' Whether he was right or wrong, it is certain that the morality of the individual is bound up in their actions towards animals. That is why Helen Jones was a woman of such natural prescience in taking her moral stance that 'welfare' was inadequate as a philosophy to protect animals. She decided she would prefer to fail than succeed on terms that were a false compromise. So Jones settled on 'rights' as the right and only course when she started her revolutionary body, ISAR. It was and remains a bellwether body.

Her stance can be contrasted with the action of the feminist Chrissie Hynde who referred during an interview with a journalist to a tale in Morrissey's *Autobiography* [2013] about her in a London pub when 'Hynde calls over a dog, lifts it on to her lap and sinks her teeth into its neck. She said, 'I'm getting a lot of attention for this since Morrissey told the world about it,' she said shrugging. 'I just wanted to experience how a bitch picks up her pups. I didn't mean to hurt it. Maybe I just bit it a little too hard.' You wonder if she would have just 'shrugged' if the bitch decided to bite her back, just so she could 'experience' how it feels.

The feminist Caitlan Moran devoted her complete column in *The Times* [2015] to a critique of her 'rescued' cat:

I am a cat hater. I hate my cat. It's taken me nine years to admit, reluctantly, that this is my emotion towards her...

I didn't hate Betty at the start. We got her and her sister from Battersea Dogs & Cats Home and I liked them both – then.

Betty – the s*** cat – was beautiful, yet oddly cold and dim.

[I sighed] "You ass-hat," before lightly chucking her off the bed...

As if she can learn nothing – even as she is flying through the air.

Honestly, I can see why Schrodinger put that cat in the box. It was because it was so f****** annoying. I wish Schrodinger had marketed Cat Boxes for us all to put our cats in. I would buy the hell out of that item.

Man, have some loyalty to our family! Do it [every dump] in next door's garden! God, I hate that cat.

Morally animals depend on humans for many aspects of their daily needs. Equally we depend on them for our daily feeds and so ultimately cause their deaths. In between those polar zones of need and death, we have to balance the inequality engendered by law towards them. To take advantage of an animal that is within our power – as all animals are – is lawful immorality in thought and deed.

Nonhuman animals:

This is an unacceptable description notwithstanding it is used for the best of reasons. An animal exists in their own right. They do not have to be compared to or justified as being a form of creature that is related to a 'human'. They do not need to justify their existence in relation to us.

However animals deserve to be treated with fairness and justice because they are living beings, not because they have 'humanlike' qualities.

We do not designate a person as a non-child or a non-man or a non-woman. We do not designate a person as non-black or non-white or non-male or non-female. We are all animals. Using the term 'non' signifies you are less than the thing you are being compared to and thereby less desirable. However we are specified it is discriminatory to classify animals in relation to humans. Animals are animals because they exist in their own right and not in comparison to us.

You do not justify fairness and justice for animals on the basis they are like men or women. Each exist in their own right. Black people are their own beings not because they are not that different to white people. It is a self-evident truth that they deserve such treatment. Precisely the same reasoning applies to animals.

Ombudswoman:

While the idea of an Ombudswoman is positive in the sense the holder would be better than an Ombudsman, nevertheless the concept is too limiting in aim and action. Therefore a more practical idea and ideal of an Animals' Advocate is preferable. For that encompasses a much wider policy which resonates with the role of a 'Defender' as one who stands up for the one they represent.

Personality:

All those within the species of homo sapiens are blessed with a 'legal personality' under English law. All animals are denied a legal personality under English law.

While there is a continuing series of applications by the Nonhuman Rights Project in America to grant animals 'personhood', there is no such application in the United Kingdom at all. Indeed even the issue of European legislation confirming that animals are 'sentient' was omitted from our legislation in plans to leave the EU.

According to the politicians, that was an oversight which will be rectified. The position remains unsatisfactory particularly given that a politicians' promise is preternaturally will-o'-the-wisp.

The English jurist Blackstone stated in his *Commentaries* [1765] that, 'Natural persons are such as the God of nature formed us; artificial are such as are created and devised by human laws for the purposes of society and government; which are called corporations or bodies politic.'

The term 'personhood' is not an ideal choice as having the word 'person' allows some curmudgeonly judge of the vanity-stricken 'Who is Bruce Springsteen?' school to take a similar churlish stance on 'Are you suggesting that this elephant is a person?' type question. It is much better to use the term 'legal personality'. Besides the fact that it is clear and straightforward, it is often also the term that is used for other natural resources such as icons and monuments and rivers. Hence it is even more apposite that it should apply to animals. For unlike other objects such as rivers and even the position of robots, the only ones that bleed and possess a personality are animals.

Property:

The idea of superiority is the base of our rights over and duty towards animals. They are our property to be used, worked and killed at will. Acceptance of this property-concept led to Martin's Act. For it protected the property rights of the owner in the animal rather than the animal itself. The same idea has permeated and is perpetuated throughout English law. The Theft Act 1968 defines 'property' as including 'money and all other property, real or personal...Wild creatures, tamed or untamed, shall be regarded as property...' Thus the animal is not deemed to count in their own right. Their status is dependent on their use to us. However the idea is not limited to English law, but affects and forms judicial thinking in its own right.

The most significant one is our need for an Advocate. That subject has a distinct advantage as it means that animals would have a legal representative in and out of court and within society. Therefore the Advocate would have a duty and responsibility to promote and protect the interests of all animals, domestic and wild. The role would be far-reaching as it would include a consideration of their need for a legal personality ['personhood'], a register of animal abusers, increased sentencing for animal abuse and a wide definition of 'abuse' that relates to all forms of suffering as opposed to 'cruelty'. The power of that position would allow the holder to examine the existing position and challenge and change it to benefit animals qua animals. Significantly, the Advocate would be charged with a primary duty of introducing an Animal Rights Act.

Such an Act would concentrate on the rights of animals as members of our society who have a value per se independent of homo sapiens and are entitled to live on their terms rather than be circumscribed by ours.

Quarantine:

In law a quarantine period was 40 days in which a woman could remain in her matrimonial home. After that period she was legally evicted. Her right to shelter vanished with her husband's death. Her protection during his life emanated from the fact that she was his 'property'. Coke, a 17th century jurist, confirmed that 'If she marry within the forty days she loseth her quarantine.' That is why the period was known as the 'widow's quarantine'.

The significance of the word has been called into play when, to prevent rabies, dogs 'coming to Britain had to spend six months in quarantine kennels'. With a resonant echo of the 2020 pandemic the Hong Kong *Standard* [1977] reported, 'A friend visited the Government Quarantine Kennels in Shatin recently and was distressed and appalled at the neglect of the poor animals awaiting their death, particularly the puppies'.

All that has changed since then as the numbers have grown exponentially while the 'wet markets' of Wuhan have become a cock-crowing weathervane for animals and us. The period of quarantine is much less as the wild animals are captured and caged before being slaughtered for the queuing customer.

After lifting the 'lockdown', in June 2020 Germany faced its biggest outbreak of Coronavirus where just over 1000 workers were tested and 'two thirds had contracted the virus'. As a result '6000 workers were put in quarantine'. The crucial point about the outbreak was not so much of the fact, but the location itself namely 'the biggest slaughterhouse'. According to *The Times* the disease had also spread to other abattoirs. The head of Tunnies, the abattoir with 30% of the German pig killing industry, helpfully explained, 'our plants aren't built for the pandemic.'

Religion:

Animals are seen as nothing less than detritus by some people who understand nothing about what really matters in life and law, be it of nature or merely the universe. We should not be surprised as religion has never been a friend of animals. For the main part it values human life too high and animal life too low. Allied to the 'trials' of animals it is significant that 'The ritual killing of animals serves an expiatory function that has been incorporated, if not explicitly sanctioned, by the Roman Catholic Church', according to the anthropologist Julio Caro Baroja.

It is a strange and unacceptable taboo in our modern society that it appears almost impossible to criticise anything about a Jew without being branded as an anti-Semite. There is a similar taboo if you dare to criticise a Muslim. Yet no one, whether Catholic or Jew or Muslim or Protestant or otherwise, are immune from criticism. Jews cannot plead for special treatment and simultaneously promote ritual slaughter. Expiatory is used in that way by Baroja so it functions as another convenient scapegoat concept. Some religions see and deem many animals as 'unclean' whether it is bees or dogs. In both Islamic and Jewish law, bees were regarded as unclean beasts; yet honey itself was not unclean. At least their principles did not offend against their palate as while bees remained dirty they were happy to eat their honey.

Rights:

The difference between 'rights' and 'welfare' is not, as many academics try to claim, a matter of semantics. The difference is fundamental to respect for an individual as an individual. That is so whether the claimant is an animal or a human. It imports the idea of dignity and possessing a right to a certain destiny rather than be subject to the whim and will of others. The difference forges an identity that starts with life and ends with death.

There is a single simple question that can be asked to decide whether the concept of rights as compared to welfare has any meaningful difference: would any free person in the world want their legal status to be defined by welfare rather than rights? Allied to that is the answer namely that we have an Animal Welfare Act. Would any free human being choose to be subject to a Human Welfare Act rather than our Human Rights Act? Would any free human being volunteer to rid themselves of their rights?

You can laugh about 'rights' for animals and some do. Even forgetting ordinary domestic pets, you can deride the idea of rights for a hedgehog or a snail. So what? Save your scorn for someone who is of no value in your mind, animal or otherwise, than dwell on the thought that someone else might well have the self-same feelings about you.

You might be reminded by the disabled lady who cared for a snail as she figured that they too have a life to lose by our conduct and destruction. In 2019 Magdalena Dusza, from Krakow, Poland, adopted a slimy pal

Misiek after spotting her in an appalling condition in a pet shop. Ever since she was a young girl she knew that she would rather have a pet snail rather than a cat or dog. Her vision and decision says more about compassion than most supposed christians.

Ritual slaughter

Religion rests on the importance of humans and the notion animals are provided for us by some deity to be used.

The Platonic idea that humans have an immortal soul was seized upon by Aristotle and became an important plank of his philosophy. Ritual slaughter is a typical example of sacrificing animals on the altar of our prejudice.

If a religion causes animals to suffer more at the point of death than the normal method of killing them in an abattoir, then there is no doubt as to the answer, there must be a change: the religious ritual must change or their diet must change. There is no valid reason to excuse such suffering on religious grounds. Indeed there is something suspect about a religion whose practitioners wish animals to undergo extra suffering at the point of death because of their own belief. It should be illegal. Why else does numerous professional veterinary organizations oppose it? Why else does the RSPCA oppose it? The reason relied upon by religious followers is neither acceptable nor humane. Far from being a taboo, it should be unlawful.

Of course, once again, it is big business and part of a money-making industry.

On a strict legal basis there is one extra salient point: why does the law allow ritual slaughter to be 'exempt' from the offence of causing an animal 'unnecessary suffering'? Given that it was initially purely on religious grounds to protect a minority who might be persecuted for their practices, it is now a multi-million pound industry at home and abroad. By making the practice exempt from the legal provision it is thereby sanctioning legal abuse. Without that exemption the ritual slaughter would be unlawful and the practitioners liable to prosecution. Besides why would you wish to adopt a religious practice that exemplifies suffering to animals?

Royalty:

The Royal Family have always had animal abuse bred in their very bones. The early English monarchy protected the wild animals and sentenced poachers to death. However, it is the reason that is telling. It was not in any way for the protection of the animals. It was for the protection of the King's property. He killed poachers so that he and he alone could enjoy the killing ritual of hunting the surviving animals to death.

It is why during the 'denial' Interview about the Epsteinconnection with a teenage girl, it is interesting and intriguing that Andrew claimed far from being with her he was spending an ordinary week-end 'shooting'. He obviously figured that blasting birds from the sky for the pleasure of killing them for fun, was the way most people spent a week-end.

It is all very well for the modern household of royalty to speak on behalf of endangered species around the world. That is valid of itself. However it would be so much better if they spoke out against their own kin's disposition to kill animals for pleasure.

Sentence:

The sentences have been and are and will remain too low unless and until new legislation is introduced which designates that animal abusers are criminals just like the ordinary common burglar or rapist or robber. Consequently the sentence should reflect that fact.

Additionally every convicted animal abuser should be banned from owning or working with animals in any capacity for life.

Slaves:

Thomas Jefferson drafted the sentence in the American Constitution that formed the principle which permeated the policies that followed:

We hold these truths to be self-evident, that all men are created equal, that they are endowed by their Creator with certain unalienable Rights, that among these are Life, Liberty and the pursuit of Happiness.

The slight problem for Jefferson was that it did not apply to any other citizens who were congenital *all men* except the all-American white man. He and the other Founding Fathers used their innate prejudice to exclude all others including women. Significantly Jefferson, like many of those brethren that were signatories, was a slave owner.

When they considered the legality of slavery, the English judges refrained from a moral analysis because they knew that no man can own another man as a matter of law or life or logic. Finally in the *Somerset Case* [1772] Lord Mansfield said, 'the man should go free.' At that moment the judge admitted a manifest truth: the man in the dock was the same as him.

Stewart's lawyer relied upon the absence of 'protection' for slaves as the base of his case. Somerset's lawyer opposed it by tellingly comparing a slave to an animal: 'upon what Principle is it – can a Man become A Dog for another Man?'

Comparing a slave to an animal was sterling advocacy as it forced Mansfield to choose between judging a man to be a mere machine and granting him his freedom. It is why he called Somerset a 'man'.

Slaves are always treated as being less than human. Slavery was abolished in England in 1807 and the colonies in 1833. Nevertheless let us not seek a false solace as pale saints when in truth we are the sinners too: we introduced slavery into America in Virginia in 1619. For our forefathers the black men and women and children were only a different species of animal. They were all seen as their 'property' being no different than the cotton they were then forced to pick. No different than the babies the women were forced to breed by their white rapist masters.

It is why Moses Finley identified in *Ancient Slavery and Modern Ideology* [1980] the reason:

> When Roman lawyers defined a slave as someone who was in the *dominium* of another, they used the quintessential property-term *dominium*. They were not dissuaded by the slave's human quality [not even when they used the word homo to refer to a slave, as they did frequently]. Nor were the millions of slave-owners who bought and sold slaves, overworked them, beat and tortured them, and sometimes put them to death, precisely as millions of horse-owners have done throughout history.

A sense of perspective can be gained by realising that for us, in one form or another, all animals remain our legal slaves.

Soul:

All humans have a soul. No animal has a soul. While that is something which is neither proven to exist or be true, it is our reason for being biased towards humans and against animals. Notwithstanding that unassailable point it allows us to be part of a human conspiracy to assume a natural superiority over all animals. Our conspiracy of silence condemns those deemed by us to be soulless.

Speciesism:

It has been long known and accepted that animals feel pain, mentally and physically as well as psychologically. If an animal is a sentient being and in some ways a kindred spirit of humans, why then are they so often treated purely as property, a thing to be owned, used or consumed? The answer lies in what Richard Ryder has termed 'speciesism' in *The Ethics of Animal Abuse* [1979]: human life being treated as having a special priority over animal life simply because it is human. That is at the root of man's assumed control and power over animals. This convenient conclusion is based on two assumptions, both borne of self-interest: we have a moral claim because of our superiority and animals are not deserving of moral rights.

Speciesism is similar to other forms of discrimination such as racism and sexism. Most of the arguments based on race and sex including biological differences, inferiority and intelligence are equally applicable to animals. Much of Western thought, in terms of philosophy and religion which was later filtered and expressed in law, was influenced by Aristotle. He believed that slaves, women and animals were inferior to freemen. Strangely though significantly it is no surprise to learn he was in the favoured superior category. Aristotle considered that 'since nature makes nothing purposeless or in vain, it is undeniably true that she has made all animals for the sake of man.' It is a self-mined streak of hubris and vainglory for one of the foremost philosophers of all time to assume a state and rely on it as a presumption without evidence and then just declare it to be true. You may as well say only humans have souls and then rely on the premise as the proof. Where is the proof for such a perverse theological notion any more than Aristotle's own?

Suffering:

Animal abuse must be defined so that all aspects of our treatment of them which affects animals in an adverse manner are within the definition. That definition must be wide in form and purpose so as to include the mental and physical and psychological abuse of animals. Whether it involves 'cruelty' or 'torture' or any graduation of those terms is not the point. The crucial point is, regardless of any degree, does it cause an animal to 'suffer' in some way. If the answer to that question is 'yes' then it should be illegal. As we are dealing with a living being that is vulnerable per se, that animal has to be able to have the advantage that the law does not permit them to be abused. Anything less is a false legal compromise borne of our desires and interests and prejudice. Being false in form means it has no value at all.

The term we must consider is not 'cruelty' which is far too narrow in context and meaning, but 'suffering'. As animals breathe and live they are entities of their own. Consequently they are entitled to be free from arbitrary suffering at the hands of and by humans. Similarly the legal term we use to create an offence is 'unnecessary suffering'. Why are we free to impose 'necessary' suffering on animals? Why does our self-imposed superiority grant us the right to abuse animals at will?

Such questions are ones we cannot escape, though by choice we do whenever we can. For our choice is governed by their birthmark curse of being without a dissenting voice.

'Cruelty' is a dead word when applied to animals and should be replaced by 'abuse'. Cruelty imports too many negative aspects of how animals are treated. It is vague and valueless. It tends to suggest an active force, though it can include an omission, by a person causing some direct harm by the form of cruelty to an animal. The word 'suffering' should be used as it is open to a wide interpretation of abuse to include the mental and physical and psychological aspects of it. Suffering covers aspects regardless of the degree of pain and the mode of abuse. Suffering takes account of the fact that the victim is vulnerable by virtue of their status within our society.

A country will easily accept lower welfare standards for animals during a transition period when leaving a trading community or during an election or trading with another nation. Cameron and May and Truss backed the idea of bringing back hunting at various stages of their careers. Then again they are all politicians. What else can we expect?

Some have openly declared they are happy to willingly engage in trade even if it means accepting the American 'lower animal welfare standards'. That alone is proof how useless welfare is as against legal rights. The latter signifies dignity that cannot be squandered by the doubtful morality of politicians. For them it is a short economic journey from China's Coronavirus pangolas to America's chlorinated chickens.

Trials:

In the past we put animals on trial because we sought a scapegoat for our own crimes and sins. If we were feckless and reckless so that we failed in our duties to protect our children and they were harmed or killed by an animal, the animal would be tried as a common criminal.

By that act we granted rights to animals and treated them as humans so we could punish them. Now we deny animals rights so we can punish them.

In 2020 the Indian authorities have practised that prescient tradition of turning animals into criminals: a Pakistani pigeon has been arrested in India for spying. They claim the number on the pigeon's leg is a secret code. Habibulluah, the owner, claims it is his phone number. In 2016 the Indian forces arrested another 'spy pigeon' which, when the truth was discovered, was closer to being a stool pigeon.

Undertaking:

Sometimes an owner will give an undertaking to the court in order to save his dog from destruction. He will agree to 'conditions' such as a lead and a muzzle. It is not enough to rely on an 'undertaking' by the owner to ensure his dog is safe in public in the future. The dog should be represented in court in their own right by an Advocate.

After all the owner may well remain feckless and reckless and fail to comply with the imposed conditions notwithstanding the undertaking was subject to his agreement. The disposition of such an owner should not be the criterion that determines the life or death of a dog.

Vivisection:

When animal experiments are reported the scientists almost always refer to mice and rats. They deliberately do so as they figure that people may care for cuddly cats and furry dogs, but they do not give a moment's thought to mice and rats. That is why mice have been mass victims of the vivisectors seeking a vaccine for the 2020 coronavirus. While there may be protests against the culling of badgers and the mass killing of squirrels, but who among us is going to defy the law for some pest let alone vermin?

That of course plays into the hands of the experimenters and vivisectionists. They always use language that is purposely vague and camouflages the abuse and suffering. An experiment conceals what is behind the statistics as the scientists conceal the truth by language and law.

We drink too much and eat too much and become ill. We smoke too much and take too many drugs and become ill. Annually we then carry out experiments and vivisection on millions of animals. Our self-engendered problems of addiction and obesity or otherwise become their problems as our natural solution.

In 2019 Nakauchi emphasised his ultimate goal: 'We don't expect to create human organs immediately, but this allows us to advance our research based upon the know-how we have gained up to this point.' The experiments will start by injecting human induced stem cells into rat and mice embryos, all of which have been genetically manipulated:

'The goal is for the rodent embryo to use the human cells to build itself a pancreas, and for two years, the team plans on watching these rodents develop and grow, carefully monitoring their organs and brains in the process. Only then will the researchers ask for approval to do the same with pigs'. That is why mice have been victims of the vivisectors seeking a vaccine to cure the coronavirus. 'While human-animal embryos have been created in the past - such as pig-human embryos and sheep-human embryos - they've never been allowed to develop to term before.'

One of the biggest fears with this type of research centres on exactly where these human stem cells actually go in an animal, and what type of cells they could develop into, once they are injected. Why does any of that matter when we can do whatever we want to those already living, as well as those yet to be born? If we are giving them life, then why should we also not deprive them of breathing?

We are guided entirely by our own ends. Vivisection is lawful because animals are deprived by us of possessing a personality and a legal representative in the form of an Advocate.

Whales:

If a country wishes to abuse animals they usually adopt a spurious excuse which they then dress up as an ecological and environmental reason. That is why Japan kills whales under the guise of science. It is nothing to do with science. It is all to do with making money. Whales are killed to make profits for the government and the community via taxes and price hikes.

Like Japan, we adopt a similar policy for the same reason when we cull badgers and cattle and squirrels and any other animal that is perceived to interfere with the shareholders' profits. As no one except the protesters seek to represent the animals subject to the cull, it is yet another reason that they need an Advocate. The alternative is to run the gamut from antelopes to zebras and every creature in between, then create a cull and kill them. In the absence of an Advocate their voice and our silence coincides.

Wife-selling:

Women were at one time legally marked as inferior from birth and merely the property of men. When in *Re Goddell* [1875] the first woman wanted to practise law in Wisconsin she was all but laughed out of court:

    The law of nature destines and qualifies the female
    sex for the bearing and nurture of the children of
    our race and for the custody of the homes of the

world…Nature has tempered woman as little for the judicial conflicts of the court room, as for the physical conflicts of the battle field…

The same prevailing view was practised in England and only changed after a lasting battle in court and society.

Allied to that is the practice of wife-selling which continued throughout England for 100 years from the 18th century until the nineteenth century. When the practice was rife, it happened because women were classified as 'chattels'. An indication of how common it was can be deduced from the fact Hardy used it in his novel, *The Mayor of Casterbridge*.

While the custom was unlawful, as it only involved men getting rid of their own unwanted property which happened to be troublesome wives, the authorities viewed it with a Nelsonian eye. A prosecution was a rare and exceptional course.

The essence of the due process was a man would line up his wife on a parade and seek the best price for her. She would have a collar and a bow just like the cattle in the market where she was sold to the highest bidder, though that was sometimes quite low. One woman was traded for 'a pint of ale and £1'. Another was rejected because the potential buyer asked 'who wants an old hen?'

As with animals, wives had a value too: 'The price of wives varied from meagre amounts to quite high sums.

Goods as well as money were exchanged. In 1832, a wife in Carlisle was sold for £1 and a Newfoundland dog.'

All of the process from the marketing to the haggling combined sexism with speciesism. The real question is the one that is never asked or answered: how many wives sold their bald, beer-bellied, bullying, drunkard, obese, philandering, triple-chinned ugly husbands? In that event which woman would be able to resist such a singularly desirable specimen?

XR:

Now more than ever is a time where people can see how jumped-up people who feel entitled to represent others and run the country are seen as naked emperors with their pants on fire. Protests on behalf of animals have garnered support across the world on a platform built by the endeavour of a small band of monkey-wrenchers from the English countryside. The policy and principle that Extinction Rebellion purveys has spread from Somerset to the coast of San Francisco, from Gloucester to the shores of Galway.

The Animal Rebellion strand of the band is more than a voice for change. They are the multiple-voices of those condemned to live and die on our terms because they are always stung by being born without a human tongue.

Yellowhammer:

This stunning member of the bunting family has suffered extreme decline over the last half a century. We have destroyed their habitat and continue to poison the countryside with pesticide. Meanwhile as with the grebe and harrier, we can add the yellowhammer to being a bird whose distinctive song has all but disappeared.

Zoo:

Zoos are parade grounds for human vanity. They have no educational value and no purpose. We have numerous ways of gaining all the information we desire and need from books and courses and documentaries and even with binoculars in the wild. The world is open to our wants to discover more about animals to satiate any didactic student in pursuit of truth. All of it is available without harming a hair on any captive animal's head.

Zoos serve no purpose. They never did except human curiosity. Now they are a morally redundant spectacle and an animal prison. A better example would be served by putting particular politicians behind bars so we could study why we have such a strange species running the country. There could be no better choice than all of our peculiar politicians. That would be a use for zoos as a start that would at least serve some purpose.

All zoos are useless animal prisons that have never served any function, except to prove we have little sense and less sensibility. They are neither educational nor interesting. All that they show is we like to be amused at someone else's expense.

They too are only another side of the same counterfeit coin that is a circus. Each only serves our purpose of showing us that animals are mere commodities, our playthings, our property. All that they entail is subservience and abuse that is sanctioned by law.

For animals, looking out from the inside, our world is a sad spectacle mixed-up of a circus and a zoo. Their suffering is the norm because we deem them to be our statistics of misery and prove why we do so. For animals our natural world is their unnatural zoo.

7

An Animals' Charter

Premise:

We hold it to be a self-evident truth that animals are created as individuals endowed with inalienable rights including life and liberty and the ability to live naturally and free from abuse by human beings.

Animals are living beings that are entitled to expect a respect from human beings.

Animals are living beings with innate dignity which must be respected by human beings who have an animal in their care or control or custody at any time.

Article 1

'Animal' means every living sentient creature other than a human being.

'Animal' includes all domestic and wild creatures at and in every stage of their development.

'Animal' includes those who are unborn and offspring and those who are dead.

'Animal' does not and cannot be interpreted to include a robot.

Article 2

Animals are entities that are entitled to a legal right to live.

Article 3

An Animals' Advocate will be appointed to initiate rights for animals.

Article 4

The Advocate will be legally qualified and represent animals in our society where their interests are actually or will potentially be affected.

Article 5

The Advocate will undertake to replace all the present legislation that affects animals with a single consolidated statute entitled the Animal Rights Act.

Article 6

The Advocate will be independent of all political parties.

Article 7

The Advocate will be independent of all organizations of a business or charitable or political or social status or otherwise.

Article 8

The Advocate will be subject to the High Court in supervising their duty and power and responsibility.

Article 9

The Advocate will possess the powers of a High Court Judge on behalf of animals.

Article 10

The Advocate will prepare an annual Report for the public and Parliament covering the actions undertaken and intended to be undertaken during that period on behalf of animals.

Article 11

The Report will be available for the public and Parliament without redactions.

Article 12

The public can request information from the Advocate who has a duty to supply such information that pertains to their responsibility for the rights of animals.

Article 13

Animals have a legal standing which enables the public to take action on their behalf before any court within the jurisdiction.

Article 14

Any member of the public can take action on behalf of animals if the information issued by the Advocate is challenged on the grounds it is incomplete or unsatisfactory.

Article 15

Any member of the public can take action on behalf of animals in the event that a Report is not issued or information requested from the Advocate is refused.

Article 16

Any member of the public can take Judicial Review and/or any other action on behalf of animals in relation to the contents of the Report or a failure to issue one.

Article 17

Any member of the public can take Judicial Review and/or any other action on behalf of animals in relation to the activities undertaken by the Advocate.

Article 18

Any member of the public can take any action on behalf of animals in relation to the failure to act in court and/or Parliament and/or any where within the jurisdiction by the Advocate in breach of their duty and responsibility.

Article 19

The Advocate will be subject to the High Court for their removal from office following Judicial Review.

Article 20

Abuse includes any act or omission that causes suffering to an animal.

Article 21

Suffering to an animal includes being treated by a human being in such a way that the animal suffers mental and/or physical and/or psychological pain of any degree or nature whether minimal or otherwise.

Article 22

Suffering to an animal includes being treated by a human being intentionally or recklessly using an animal to cause suffering to another animal in any manner or place whatsoever.

Article 23

Suffering to and causing pain to an animal includes a human being acting directly or indirectly and/or being an agent for any other person whether for payment or otherwise.

Article 24

Suffering to and causing pain includes a human being acting directly or indirectly and/or using an agent and/or any other person whether for payment or otherwise.

Article 25

Suffering to and causing pain includes a human being acting directly or indirectly by using an agent and/or any other person to cause such pain.

Article 26

Suffering to and causing pain includes a human being acting directly or indirectly by using an agent and/or any other animal to cause such pain.

Article 27

Suffering to and causing pain includes a human being acting directly or indirectly by using an agent and/or any other person and/or an animal to cause such pain.

Article 28

Suffering to and causing pain to an animal includes the animal that suffers and/or the animal causing the said suffering.

Article 29

The animal which suffers includes any animal that is caused to suffer and/or the animal that causes such suffering.

Article 30

All experiments carried out for research which cause suffering to animals are hereby illegal.

Article 31

An animal cannot be subject to an experiment unless it is for veterinary treatment for that specific animal that has a medical condition that requires to be treated.

Article 32

An animal cannot be subject to an experiment for research and/or a medical condition of any nature whatsoever relating to a human being.

Article 33

Any experiment on an animal except for veterinary treatment relating to the said animal is subject to permission being granted in writing by the Advocate.

Article 34

Any experiment granted by the Advocate is subject to Judicial Review by any member of the public in respect of any said permission granted for any experiment of any nature on any animal at any time.

Article 35

Suffering includes abandoning an animal that a person has in their care or control or custody at any time whatsoever regardless of ownership and/or under a contract and/or otherwise.

Article 36

Suffering includes abandoning an animal that a person has in their care and control and custody whether that possession is lawful or unlawful.

Article 37

Abandoning an animal is an offence whereby the said abandonment is an intentional or reckless act or omission.

Article 38

Suffering to and causing pain to an animal includes depriving an animal of sustenance of any nature whatsoever whether it is minimal or otherwise.

Article 39

Suffering by deprivation of sustenance includes depriving an animal of drink or food or any comfort that interferes with their mental and/or physical and/or psychological condition.

Article 40

All forms of hunting where that directly or indirectly involves setting an animal on another animal is hereby illegal.

Article 41

All forms of hunting where that directly or indirectly involves setting an animal on another animal and/or involving a human being is hereby illegal.

Article 42

All forms of hunting where it directly or indirectly involves arranging for the setting of an animal on another animal and/or involving a human being is hereby illegal.

Article 43

All forms of the said hunting in any form whatsoever where it involves a domestic and/or wild animal and/or a human being is hereby illegal.

Article 44

All forms of the said hunting in any form whatsoever where it involves intentionally and/or recklessly setting any animal on any other animal and/or a human being are hereby illegal.

Article 45

Eating an animal except in the case of necessity causes suffering to an animal and is hereby illegal.

Article 46

Any person relying on the defence of necessity in causing suffering to any animal at any time has the burden of proof of establishing that defence.

Article 47

Anyone who eats an animal and/or causes an animal to be eaten whether by a human being and/or an animal and claims necessity must satisfy the court on the evidential burden of proof which is on the defence.

Article 48

Where a person is in danger from an attack and/or is being attacked by an animal and/or another animal is in such danger it is subject to a reliance on self-defence in causing suffering including death to the said animal must satisfy the court on the evidential burden of proof on the defence.

Article 49

Culling of any animal for economic or political or social reasons or otherwise is illegal.

Article 50

Where culling is claimed to be necessary by any person and/or body including the government for other than economic or political or social reasons or otherwise it is subject to the consent of the Advocate who can reject the claim if it is contrary to law.

Article 51

Where culling is claimed to be necessary the burden of proof rests on the person and/or body seeking the consent of the Advocate to the criminal standard that it is not contrary to law.

Article 52

Where culling is rejected by the Advocate the claimant can appeal to the High Court.

Article 53

Where culling is granted by the Advocate any member of the public can appeal to the High Court in respect of that permission being granted.

Article 54

If an animal has to be killed for any legal reason it has to be undertaken with the care and preservation of dignity that is adopted towards a human being approaching death.

Article 55

An animal that appears as an exhibit before a court is entitled to a fair trial and must be represented by the Advocate during the proceedings.

Article 56

The right of an animal subject to court proceedings to be represented by the Advocate is independent of the said animal being abandoned or owned or otherwise.

Article 57

The Advocate will represent an animal in all civil and criminal matters including before a tribunal whatever the subject of the proceedings.

Article 58

All civil and criminal matters includes courts that adjudicate upon family issues and immigration and employment tribunals and disciplinary actions and otherwise where the rights of any animal is being subject to a judgment of any description.

Article 59

Where an animal appears as an exhibit before a court and the proceedings are adjourned they are entitled to be released on bail until the following hearing.

Article 60

Animals that are protected by the Animal Rights Act 2020 are entitled to act and enjoy conditions consistent with the Future Freedoms and endorsed by the Advocate.

Article 61

Wild animals living in the wild must be allowed to live according to their nature in the natural world and not be subject to interference with their inclination by human beings.

Article 62

Zoos and similar businesses admitting the public whether by payment or free cause confined animals whether in a cage or otherwise to suffer and are hereby illegal.

Article 63

The Five Freedoms are replaced by a Future Freedoms Memorandum covering the duties and responsibilities that human beings have towards animals which are incorporated in a legal code specifying the role and status of animals.

Article 64

The Future Freedoms applies to all animals and are concerned with rights such that the moral and ethical treatment of animals is a legal duty and responsibility.

Article 65

Where in an action or claim in any court or tribunal is by an animal they must be represented by the Advocate regardless of ownership or possession or otherwise of the said animal.

Article 66

Any entertainment or experiment or enterprise that would be unlawful if undertaken in relation to a human being without their written consent is illegal unless the animal is represented by the Advocate who grants express written consent on their behalf.

Article 67

Any member of the public can take legal action against the Advocate if they claim such consent has been unfairly and/or unreasonably granted and is thereby contrary to law.

Article 68

As all forms of life co-exist within an interdependent ecosystem the legal protection for animals must incorporate that ethos and be endorsed by the Advocate.

Article 69

Animal rights within the Animal Rights Act are not subject to any ethnic or philosophical or religious exemptions whatsoever now and hereafter.

Article 70

Ritual slaughter in any form whether based on ethnicity or philosophy or religion or otherwise whatsoever is illegal.

Article 71

Future policy discussions by governments that affect animal rights are subject to representations from the Advocate and/or the public.

Article 72

Future policy discussions by governments that affect animal rights are subject to legal action if the representations from the Advocate and/or the public are not implemented.

Article 73

Research will be used for the future protection of animal rights as knowledge of sentience of all species is gained.

Article 74

Countries that practise animal abuse will not be traded with unless and until they promote animal rights legislation comparable with English law.

Article 75

Animals that are subject to abuse in other countries will not be exported to them unless and until they reduce their suffering by legislation comparable with English law.

Article 76

Animals that are subject to abuse in other countries will not be imported from them unless and until they reduce their suffering by legislation comparable with English law.

Article 77

The legislation and standards attained by other countries on animal rights shall be recognized and adopted where they are superior to English law.

Article 78

All member countries of the United Kingdom must adopt legislation to treat animals in accordance with the principles of this Charter.

Article 79

Language that is discriminatory towards animals and/or people that derive directly or indirectly from animals is hereby unlawful.

Article 80

Confining animals in their custody by limiting their movement in any form or manner whether caged or enclosures or otherwise are hereby illegal.

Article 81

Angling by catching and hooking fish by any form whatsoever and whether in or out of a man-made lake or natural environment or water as a business or hobby or pastime or otherwise is hereby illegal.

Article 82

Circuses confining and training animals in their custody and under their control whether caged or otherwise for public entertainment are hereby illegal.

Article 83

Dog racing using animals under their control and in their custody is hereby illegal.

Article 84

Horse racing using animals for every stage of training and running and jumping fences for public entertainment whether for award or betting or charity or otherwise is hereby illegal.

Article 85

Animals used for entertainment and pastimes and sport using animals performing for human beings that directly or indirectly cause suffering to an animal whether for payment of any kind whatsoever or otherwise is hereby illegal.

Article 86

Any activity whether as an exchange or a gift or free or for payment or otherwise using animals that directly or indirectly cause suffering is hereby illegal.

Article 87

Films that portray animal abuse involving an animal and/or with another animal and/or with a human causing suffering on screen whether real or fake are hereby unlawful.

Article 88

Legal Aid for action to represent the rights of animals is available to the Advocate.

Article 89

Legal Aid to represent the rights of animals is available to the public to take action against the Advocate in respect of the said rights.

Article 90

Legal Aid to represent the rights of animals is available to the public to lodge a private prosecution against any authority whether a private business or local council or government department or otherwise that is in breach of animal rights legislation and/or this Charter.

Article 91

The sentence for those convicted of animal abuse whatsoever is a maximum term of 14 years' imprisonment under the Animal Rights Act 2020.

Article 92

The sentence for those convicted of any offence of animal abuse automatically includes being deprived of the care and control and custody of all animals for life.

Article 93

The age of criminal responsibility applies to all offences of animal abuse where the person intentionally or recklessly by act or omission causes suffering to any animal contrary to the Animal Rights Act 2020.

Article 94

A judge undertakes special training on the nature of animal abuse before they can carry out trials and/or sentencing of defendants charged with and/or convicted of the said abuse.

Article 95

For the avoidance of doubt where the offence of animal abuse has been committed by a person who is 16-years-old or younger the adult responsible for the care and control and custody of the said person is vicariously liable for the offence under the Animal Rights Act 2020 as well as the person committing the said offence.

Article 96

The Animal Rights Act 2020 will be based upon the equivalent statute that applies to humans namely the Human Rights Act 1998.

Article 97

The Animal Rights Act 2020 will incorporate the principles of the Human Rights Act 1998 in particular the rights applying to that latter Act by the European Convention on Human Rights and Fundamental Freedoms 1950.

Article 98

The Animal Rights Act 2020 will protect animals from discrimination and prejudicial treatment that causes them any form of suffering of any nature whatsoever that would equally apply to humans under the Human Rights Act 1998.

Article 99

Animals are granted a legal personality consistent with the principles of this Charter and under the Animal Rights Act 2020.

Article 100

Ecocide which causes any damage whether temporary or permanent to the planet by contamination or destruction or pollution or otherwise that thereby results in any suffering to any animal directly or indirectly is hereby declared an offence within the Animal Rights Act 2020.

8

Yesterday's Child

During the warm summer holidays two schoolboys decided to buy a gerbil. The boys, who were 11 and 13 years-old, were cousins. They had saved and pooled their pocket money for a particular purpose. They had over £6.

They went to the local pet shop together where gerbils were for sale at £2 each.

They bought a gerbil and took it to the older boy's home. They had one thing in mind: they intended to kill the purchased pet.

They placed the gerbil in the garden.

Then the cousins got an inflammable aerosol which they used as a blowtorch intending to torch the gerbil to death. The gerbil tried to escape from the flames. One of the boys threw a brick at the creature which hit the gerbil and wounded her. They then took it in turns to fry the gerbil alive until she burned to death.

The boys then threw the burned body away.

The next day they went back to the pet shop together and bought another gerbil.

They took him to a nearby park as they intended to kill him. First they attempted to drown the creature by throwing him into the river. Evidently the gerbil did not die quickly enough. So they dragged him out of the river when he was only half-drowned. Then they impaled him on a stick. As he was then wounded too, they threw him back into the river to drown.

The next day they went back to the pet shop together and bought another gerbil.

This time they took her to the younger boy's home.

They placed the gerbil in the garden.

Then the cousins got some white spirit and poured it all over the gerbil. They then set the creature alight. Both boys watched while the animal was being burned alive. Evidently the gerbil did not die quickly enough. They saw that one of her legs was still moving. So they repeated their action and poured more white spirit all over her. Then they torched the gerbil again.

This time they were successful so they threw the charred carcass away.

They did not visit the pet shop again as by then they had spent all their pocket money.

The abuse of the gerbils was discovered and investigated. Neither of the boys could give any reason for their actions. The most revealing insight into their intentions was that one had initially said to the other, 'I feel like killing something.'

That was in 1987. Considering the path of violence well-trodden by other animal abusers including the Boston Strangler and Ted Bundy and Ian Brady, who knows of the fate and the progress of the cousins in 2020?

Over the past three decades, given the knowledge we now have as to the proclivities that animal abusers possess, what was and is their future? How did they act towards other animals and people? In the scheme of the nature of the perpetrator's deeds of such abuse there is every reason to believe they would target other vulnerable victims. The links in the chain are already forged between the yesterday's gerbil-killers and their potential to be tomorrow's badger-baiters and wife-beaters. Who would be optimistic their penchant for animal abuse would end with the deaths of the three gerbils?

The connection between animal abuse and child abuse is accentuated by the fact those who abuse animals as children often graduate to use violence on people. In 2012 a boy put a neighbour's cat in a microwave oven. As the boy was eight-years-old he was below the age of criminal responsibility. He is a potentially dangerous child who with time might turn to violent crime. How will he behave in 2020 and hereafter?

The Anti-social Behaviour, Crime and Policing Act 2014 has underlined the relevance of the character of the owner and has even balanced it against the character of the dog. Therefore the court should hold the good character of the owner in favour of his dog. Conversely the court should not hold his bad character against his dog. It is a stronger reason not to kill his dog if the defendant has used his violent nature to change the creature's character. Otherwise that would mean the dog is a victim twice over, once by his owner and then by the law.

A chilling confession by Anthony Stravato is a warning to the authorities and the community. He served eight months in prison for offences including torturing and mutilating and killing his mother's cat. Stravato boasted on Facebook that: 'as n ill be tha next serial killer since i have a serial killer trait. im sure i knew it already. i used to watch my cats die all tha time when i was young so i began to be fasinated with death when i was 6.' (*sic*)

When he was asked why he 'keeps killing animals' he said, 'yes i do like it i enjoyed it.' (*sic*)

Stravato is a registered Level 3 sex offender which means he is highly likely to re-offend. That was in 2016. How can any animal be safe anywhere that is visited by Stravato in 2020 or hereafter? How can any animal within his vicinity or vision ever avoid being a fateful future victim of Stravato?

9

An Animals' Charter: The Future

Law can show us what is real and what is not in relation to human affairs. Law has a power that is positive when it is used for the good of the community. Law is justice in action.

In *Nair v. Union of India* [2000] the judge in the Indian High Court delivered a judgment that promoted the end of the circus by using the principle of law with justice at its core. Narayana Kurup J said:

In conclusion, we hold that circus animals are being forced to perform unnatural tricks, are housed in cramped cages, subjected to fear, hunger, pain, not to mention the undignified way of life they have to live with no respite and the impugned notification has been issued in conformity with the changing scenario, values of human life, philosophy of the Constitution, prevailing conditions and the surrounding circumstances to prevent the infliction of unnecessary pain or suffering on animals. Though not homo sapiens, they are also beings entitled to dignified existences and humane treatment sans cruelty and torture.

Many believe that the lives of humans and animals are equally valuable and that their interest should count equally...

If humans are entitled to fundamental rights, why not animals?

In our considered opinion, legal rights shall not be the exclusive preserve of the humans which has to be extended beyond people thereby dismantling the thick legal wall with humans all on one side and all non-human animals on the other side.

While the law currently protects wildlife and endangered species from extinction, animals are denied rights, an anachronism which must necessarily change.

Kurup is right. Justice is indivisible. There is no reason why animals should be denied the protection of the mantle of law and indeed every reason for it to apply to them. Wherever they are harmed by us and suffer from abuse they are 'entitled' to be protected. A law that fails to protect animals from us is edentulous.

Law protects the underdog. Animals have always been our underdogs' underdog yet are denied legal protection from us when we decide to deliberately cause them "necessary suffering". Whatever we gain in material terms will prove how short-sighted we are as our loss will be calculated by the scales of blind justice. A world without animals would be a world without vision: for in that failure to see what matters dung beetles are the lodestar of our law.

How long can we fail to see that animals should be respected by being granted 'rights'? Who could take Descartes seriously anyway when you learn he was a dyed-in-the-wool vivisectionist? How could he be anything else? He was the ancestor of Pavlov who tortured dogs for fun. Then when they barked through fear while being literally scared to death, their howls irritated Pavlov. His answer was to remove their voice box so he was not troubled by the awful sound which assaulted his ears. Pavlov was such a sensitive scientist that he could not bear the hear the sounds of the animals' suffering that he had deliberately caused. Pavlov conveniently found solace in the sound of silence as he then did not have any reminder of his calculated violence. Is he less than our own reflection?

The growth of robots has prompted an academic growth in research on their legal position. Many lawyers and scientists are calling for robots to be granted a status akin to a legal personality. The Members of the European Parliament [MEPs] endorsed the theory during a debate on the strict rules of how humans interact with machines so that they can be held accountable for any harm they do. The MEPs showed their own brand of political wisdom by describing robots as 'electronic persons'.

There is also the reality and role of 'unethical robots'

that possess the ability to pull a trigger on a weapon which could kill a person. The concept has now captured the imagination of an English Supreme Court Judge, Lord Hodge, who has initiated an investigation into their legal position.

Perhaps it is timely as in 2019 an electric car in America would not open its doors after it crashed. The driver inside was burned alive. Who caused the death of the driver? Was it the manufacturer? Was it the owner of the robotic vehicle?

Animals are not even part of the discussion. Yet unlike a pile of mangled metal that at worst merely rusts, animals at least breathe and bleed.

Moreover, when animals are discussed by judges they are often belittled as of no consequence or simply outside the judicial circle of compassion. In the *Kiko Case* [2015] an application for 'personhood' in America was dismissed by a unanimous decision which included Associate Judge Fahey. Later Fahey 'struggled with' his decision and then delivered his 'Opinion':

> To treat a chimpanzee as if he or she had no right to liberty protected by habeas corpus is to regard the chimpanzee as entirely lacking independent worth, as a mere resource for human use, a thing the value of which consists exclusively in its usefulness to others. Instead, we should consider whether a chimpanzee is an individual with inherent value who has the right to be treated with respect

Fahey relied on Regan's 'respect principle' to set out his judicial confusion yet failed to answer the moral question as Regan's concept is clear:

> The following principle *(the respect principle)* does this: *We are to treat those individuals who have inherent value in ways that respect their inherent value...*an egalitarian, nonperfectionist interpretation of formal justice...It enjoins us to treat *all* those individuals having inherent value in ways that respect their value, and thus it requires respectful treatment of all who satisfy the subject-of-a-life criterion. Whether they are moral agents or patients, we must treat them in ways that respect their equal inherent value.

Instead of being fearless, Fahey confessed his perverse personal dilemma:

> 'Since we first denied leave to the Nonhuman Rights Project ...I have struggled with whether this was the right decision. Although I concur with the Court's decision to deny leave now I continue to question whether the court was right to deny leave in the first instance. The issue...is profound and far-reaching...we will not be able to ignore it. While it may be arguable that a chimpanzee is not a "person", there is no doubt that it is not merely a thing.'

It is peculiar that knowing an animal is not a 'thing' should cause Fahey to wring his judicial hands as if the issue was beyond a solution when he had these options: he could have delivered a discerning dissenting judgment and declared animals are equally legally more than pure property.

Nevertheless Fahey was so troubled by the question of animal sentience he attempted to share his 'dilemma' with his brother judges in the *Kiko Case*:

> Does an intelligent nonhuman animal who thinks and plans and appreciates life as human beings do have a right to the protection of the law against arbitrary cruelties and enforced detentions visited on him or her? This is not merely a definitional question, but a deep dilemma of ethics and policy that demands our attention.

Fahey's Opinion is hailed as a prescient sign for the future of animal rights. That is wrong. His view is a failure: it is jejune jurisprudence based on a weakness of spirit and a failure to make a decision based on an ethical vision. Why does Fahey care what the other judges think? Why did he follow the unanimous decision to dismiss the case? Why did he not have the strength to dissent?

Fahey's stance is pointless and pusillanimous as he looked at animals through our mirror of morality but failed to reflect on their suffering and failed to be fearless when he had the chance. Why did he not have the courage of his judicial conviction? Is the fault 'The inadequacy of the law' as he claims or just Fahey's reflective judicial conscience? Is it no less than a self-inflicted inadequacy?

Dodo Justice:

Law is the only moral system that can save animals from their lifetime perennial enemies. All the philosophical discussions in the world will not save animals for us and from us. They are entitled to live freely in a world they choose with or without us as they count in their own right. Well-meaning discussions about the consequences of a world without animals are ultimately just verbal smoke rings unless and until the ideas are enshrined in law. Justice is at the root of saving us from a world without animals. Why is it so hard for us to simply let them be? To live with whatever risk that involves according to the ultimate law, that of nature, given that ours has failed them? Why do we insist on a caveman existence in our legal treatment of animals in the 21st century?

What is the value of justice to animals? They cannot read or write or vote or engage in anything close to registering a protest, save for a final kick before being forced towards destiny's cell. Such a view though understandable is misguided. Justice is simply the quality of being just. Justice is performing the right action for the right reason at the right time. Justice is noble because it does not depend on what is lost or gained by those dispensing it, but the value to those receiving it. Justice is embodied in the Magna Carta so we can render what is due to a person and show the same spirit to an animal. Justice is an aspiration and sometimes even an attainment.

The future of animals depends upon our common law. In the end what is the difference between an attorney and an animal except for innumerable murmurings of each though as to which one makes the more melliloquent sound it is often difficult to discern.

An Advocate would examine the existing position and change it to benefit animals qua animals. An Animal Rights Act would concentrate on animals as members of our society who have a value per se and are entitled to live on their terms rather than be circumscribed by ours.

Property and Personality:

It is one point to be the voice of those who need help because they are inarticulate or vulnerable or weak or indeed all those things. Nevertheless they at least have a voice of their own and an ability to show their state and what they need, be it personally or vicariously. Then their case can be analysed, their needs taken into account, then decided on its merits. Being human with rights means you are entitled to be treated with respect and rectitude and your claim and you receive the dignity you deserve. Then whatever the result or verdict the judge and jury deliver, all those affected can rest easy in the belief that justice has been done. However it is quite another thing altogether when you are designated to be a thing as a matter of law. Then because you are voiceless you remain outside the law. That is no less than justice denied because those in power have a power over you as the powerless. Your fortune and future then forever depends upon their sense of innate fairness as your right to remain alive or otherwise does not exist. As a result of that position and reasoning the Whanganui River was granted 'a legal personality' in New Zealand in 2017 after a 140-year battle. Why is the blood of an animal less worthy legally than the flow of a river?

Masters of the Universe:

Our relationship with animals was considered in *R. v. Menard* [1978] by the Quebec Court of Appeal where Lamer JA said:

On the other hand, the animal is inferior to man, and takes its place within a hierarchy which is the hierarchy of animals, and above all is part of nature with all its "racial and natural" selections. The animal is subordinate to nature and to man. It will often be in the interests of man to kill and mutilate wild or domestic animals, to subjugate them and, to this end, to tame them with all the painful consequence this may entail for them and, if they are too old, or too numerous, or abandoned, to kill them.

This explanation denies rights to animals and denotes our duties towards them when it is considered necessary to control human behaviour. So in the legal sense the animal as a defendant is tried by a human prosecutor and a human judge and jury. The animal has neither a defence counsel nor a defence. Nor can the animal ever have a defence. For the crime the animal has committed is solely being born and the figurative trial is a denial of natural justice.

The words used by Lamer underline the reasons why animals are exploited. So there was no possible doubt about it he explained in detail that animals are in 'our world' and so any protection given to them is a result of 'The responsibilities that we impose on ourselves as their masters.' His judgment was no less than legal speciesism based on the misguided morals of Aristotle.

Polar Positions:

However there is nothing surprising about Lamer's view. For the tone and bias only echoes English law. In 1895 a society formed to promote the abolition of vivisection was held to be charity. The judge said, 'Cruelty is degrading to man and its suppression advances morals and education among men'. That view did not persuade the judges in England's then highest court. The House of Lords reversed that decision in *National Anti-vivisection Society* [1948] holding that the abolition was outweighed by the advantages of its continuance: 'It would destroy a source of enormous blessings to mankind. That is a positive and calamitous detriment of appalling magnitude'.

In truth there are two stark polar positions at play in respect of vivisection namely (a) animals are unlike us and so any experiment is likely to produce an unreliable result and hence morally should not be undertaken at all or (b) animals are so like us they will be subject to such pain it is morally unacceptable to cause them to undergo any experiment. It follows that we do it because our might makes it right.

Feral soul:

We have moved from being anthropomorphic to anthropocentric by using our might to prove we are right. If we end up with a world without bees that would be a symbol our law as our symbol of morality has failed. While such a world sounds extreme it is now in our vision.

Most human beings now have 'rights' because they are human beings. In essence these allow a person to act freely providing he does not infringe another's rights. These have arisen because of our self-serving special status as a rational, sentient being. However in formulating and granting these rights, they have not been limited to humans who are rational. Rights extend to all within the category of homo sapiens. But that is the limit. We have chosen deliberately to deny those rights to animals. Therefore the same practice may be legal or illegal according to the victim and the profit to us.

Our failure to protect animals from us is a self-defeating act ensuring a Pyhrric victory for profit over ethics where the weak perish on the altar of our avarice. We squander the lives of animals for a monetary mirage when we should be staring into a mirror of our own morality. Then we will save animals for a world that needs them more than we need to practise greed. Our decision depends as much on our vision as on our understanding of law. For as with the soul of a single cow, it is a truth both rare and raw that feral justice is the soul of our common law.

When you consider how law has grown there is no escape from the belief that belief in the religious sense has permeated its sinews. It is why the idea that we have a soul whilst animals do not has fixed our superiority and the consequent inferiority of animals.

Yet the notion is based on a notion that has no validity at all. It is naked prejudice that enables us to practise abuse because our strength overpowers their birthmark curse of being born an animal. However Reza Aslan in *God: A Human History of Religion* [2018] details the true position:

Where did the idea of the soul come from?

The truthful answer is we don't know...It is the result of something far more primal and difficult to explain: our ingrained, intuitive, and wholly experiential belief that we are, whatever else we are, embodied souls.

Our quest in the following chapters is neither to prove nor to disprove the existence of the soul (there is no proof either way).

That has to be considered and taken into account in relation to the view of Clarence Darrow in *Verdicts Out of Court* [1963] where he explores the myth of the soul:

It is impossible to draw the line between inorganic matter and the simpler forms of plant life, and equally impossible to draw the line between plant life and animal life, or between other forms of animal life and what we human beings are pleased to call the highest form. If the thing which we call "life" is itself the soul, then cows have souls; and, in the very nature of things, we must allow souls to all forms of life and to inorganic matter as well.

Aslan and Darrow are both right. Our problem in promoting prejudice towards animals by law is self-engendered. As with all aspects of prejudice, it has neither sense nor sensibility on its side because it is not derived from a logical base. The result stems from a caveman philosophy and ends in a dodo justice. While it is convenient for us to continue with a conspiracy of complacency, our lack of logic and compassion detracts from our law.

We gain by the pain inflicted on an innocent unwilling victim. That is inhumane and unethical. Granting animal rights will in turn strengthen human rights. Ultimately the fate of animals and us is inextricably linked. In the mystery of living our destinies are interdependent and interrelated and interwoven. That self-evident truth should be reflected in our mirror of morality which is law.

Law is the universal language of natural justice. Much as a slave needed to be freed from his owner, animals need a legal personality. For that status alone guarantees the quintessence of natural justice that rights run with life itself. In the *Somerset v. Stewart* [1772], involving a claim by the master for his runaway slave, the court had to determine whether slavery was legal in England. Lord Mansfield CJ laid the foundation stone of its abolition:

'The state of slavery is of such a nature, that it is incapable of being introduced on any reasons, moral or political; but only by positive law...It is so odious, that nothing can be suffered to support it, but positive law...I cannot say this case is allowed or approved by the law of England; and therefore the black must be discharged.'

Abraham Lincoln said, 'I am in favour of animal rights as well as human rights.' That is the way of a whole human being. As the President and a practising lawyer he saw the law as it was and as it should be.

Dovetailing their ideas with an unassailable truth, Darwin said, 'Animals, whom we have made our slaves, we do not like to consider our equal.' When Salt's classic work, *Animals' Rights*, was reviewed by a Victorian feminist, Edith Ward, she stated in the aptly-named *Shafts* [1892], 'the case for the animal is the case of the woman. What [is] more likely to impress mankind with the necessity of justice for women than the awakening of the idea that justice was the right of even an ox or a sheep?'

Isonomy has no meaning or purpose if equality applies to humans alone. Philosophical discussions about rights are as valueless as verbal smoke-rings fading into thin air unless and until animals possess a defined legal status. If it is right that we can assume a superior role over animals and then treat or ill-treat them accordingly, then the law is wrong. Animals are entitled by virtue of being alive and sentient to the reciprocal protection within the mantle of law. It is not that they breathe the same air as us that matters, but that they breathe to have life. Justice for animals is rooted in their very existence.

Narayanakurup J in the *Balakrishnan Case* in the Indian High Court discerned our lawful negativity towards animals. His evaluation was and remains a universal lodestone judgment:

'Legal rights shall not be the exclusive preserve of the humans which has to be extended beyond people thereby dismantling the thick legal wall with humans all on one side and all non-human animals on the other side...animals are denied rights, an anachronism which must necessarily change.'

That wall is the equivalent of the Berlin Wall which denied the people behind it the twin limbs of freedom and justice. Unlike that wall, the one we have constructed between animals and us applies injustice throughout the world. The legal wall we have conspiratorially constructed between animals and us is built with bricks of natural injustice.

English Law is shamed by its innate myopia in failing to respect animals as compared to the principles endorsed by Radhakrishnan J in the *Animal Welfare Board Case* [2014] in the Indian Supreme Court. His interpretation is a signpost for their future:

We may, at the outset, indicate unfortunately, there is no international agreement that ensures the welfare and protection of animals. United Nations, all these years, safeguarded only the rights of human beings, not the rights of other species like animals, ignoring the fact that many of them, including Bulls, are sacrificing their lives to alleviate human suffering, combating disease and as food for human consumption. International community should hang their head in shame, for not recognizing their rights all these ages, a species which served the humanity from the time of Adam and Eve.

When our gain is measured by the pain inflicted on a vulnerable victim, it is unethical to continue the practice. Animals need to be freed from our legal yoke. Only natural justice as the quintessence of law can promote the self-evident truth we are all animals-in-law.

Animals need an artificial personality precisely because like us they are not artificial. Animals deserve an artificial personality as a matter of law because like us they are real. Jurisprudentially a legal system that fails to protect vulnerable victims promotes the letter and spirit of injustice. In facing that charge English Law has provided the evidence to find itself 'Guilty'.